Inside the
Sunday Gospels

New Commentaries
for the Year of Matthew
Year A

Inside the
Sunday Gospels

New Commentaries
for the Year of Matthew
Year A

Peta Sherlock

E.J. Dwyer

For the parishioners of St Andrew's Clifton Hill with
St Luke's North Fitzroy who have read and lived this Gospel with me.

First published in 1995 by
E.J. Dwyer (Australia) Pty Ltd
Unit 13, Perry Park
33 Maddox Street
Alexandria NSW 2015
Australia
Phone: (02) 550-2355
Fax: (02) 519-3218

National Library of Australia
Cataloguing-in-Publication data

Sherlock, Peta, 1946–

   Inside the Sunday Gospels: new commentaries for the year of Matthew, year A.

   ISBN 0 85574 174 0.

   1. Bible. N.T. Matthew—Criticism, interpretation, etc.
   2. Bible. N.T. Matthew—Homiletical use.
   3. Bible. N.T. Matthew—Liturgical lessons, English.
   4. Bible. N.T. Matthew—Commentaries. I. Title.

   251.08

Cover and text design by Anaconda Graphic Design
Cover illustration, St Matthew, Evangelist, Monastery Hillander, 14th century, from St Matthew's Anglican
Church, Ashburton, Vic, reproduced with permission.
Typeset in Perpetua 12/14 pt by A to Z Distributors
Printed in Australia by Alken Press, Smithfield, N.S.W.

10 9 8 7 6 5 4 3 2 1
99 98 97 96 95

Distributed in the United States by:
   Morehouse Publishing
   871 Ethan Allen Highway
   RIDGEFIELD CT 06877
   Ph: (203) 431-3927
   Fax: (203) 431 3964
Distributed in Canada by:
   Meakin and Associates
   Unit 17
   81 Auriga Drive
   NEPEAN, ONT K2E 7Y5
   Ph: (613) 226 4381
   Fax: (613) 226 1687

Distributed in Ireland and the U.K. by:
   Columba Book Service
   93 The Rise
   Mount Merrion
   BLACKROCK CO. DUBLIN
   Ph: (01) 283-2954
   Fax: (01) 288-3770
Distributed in New Zealand by:
   Catholic Supplies (NZ) Ltd
   80 Adelaide Road
   WELLINGTON
   Ph: (04) 384 3665
   Fax: (04) 384 3663

PREFACE

I think I learn best by working with the scriptures themselves, by asking my questions of the text. In this book of commentaries on Year A of the Revised Common Lectionary, I continue my explorations into the vast area of biblical hermeneutics, focused on the distinctive features of Matthew's Gospel.

I have been pleased to find the parables of Jesus, as well as the long stories of the characters who meet with Jesus in John's Gospel, playing a significant part in these comments. I am not the first, and I will not be the last, to recognize the power of story. I have been humbled again and again by the gracious way that Jesus used stories, his willingness to let go of the meaning, and trust his audience. Truth is pleased to meet us on our territory. So I will happily continue my refusal to explain every story I ever tell. Anyway, someone has said that explaining a story is like explaining a joke.

Some days I feel very close to the text of scripture, as if it has been written directly for me. In hermeneutical terms, the horizons merge or fuse. But that can be dangerous for both me and the text. I domesticate the text and only hear what I want to hear from it. When my questions alone set the agenda, the text ceases to challenge me and set me free, and such words are hardly worth sharing with others.

Some days I feel incredibly distant from the text, separated by half a world of time and space, language and culture. Some scholars have argued that the goal of interpretation or translation is to give us "a new land on which to disembark."[1] But the text can thus become so tied to its own culture that it becomes irrelevant to me and functions only as a distant memory of a far-off faith.

Walter Wink[2] gives us the clue that there is a third way of relating to the text which is neither fusion, nor distance, but communion, a kind of creative tension between the two. I bring my questions to the text, being as open as I can be about my prejudices and preconceived ideas. But I find that the answers I hear from this classic text make me go back and rewrite my entire list of questions, revise my agenda. Or, even more strangely, when I am feeling further from the text than ever before, suddenly I will have a moment of insight in which God speaks to me precisely in the distancing. A spiral of understanding has begun, which will end in heaven, when at last we will know as we are known.

And so this grace of Jesus, the storyteller who lets the listeners have their head, finally challenges me to be a gracious reader and give the meaning back to its author. The question, whether I listen to the text or argue with it, is not so important after all. It seems to me that the text doesn't really mind which starting point I choose. The greater danger for this day and age is to ignore the text completely. I hope it will remain clear in these commentaries that, even when I am in my fiercest arguing mode, I do love and deeply respect this gracious text and the God I know through these scriptures.

1. Marcia Falk, *Love Lyrics from the Bible: A Translation and Literary Study of the Song of Songs,* Almond Press, Sheffield, 1982, 54-5.

2. *The Bible in Human Transformation: Towards a New Paradigm for Biblical Study,* Fortress Press, Philadelphia, 1973, 19.

Many of these commentaries first appeared in the
national Australian newspaper, *Church Scene,* and are used here with the
kind permission of its editor, Gerald Davis.

The readings are those set in the Revised Common Lectionary for Year A, the Year of Matthew. The Gospel portions are very similar to those found in the Three Year Lectionary already in use in many churches. Where there are widely differing readings, I have provided comments on both passages or referred to another Sunday. The Lectionary aims to read through the Gospel according to Matthew, with passages from John's Gospel used in the Easter season. During Advent and Lent passages are chosen to suit the theme of the day. These Lectionaries do not cover all of Matthew, but do include the parts that are distinctive to this Gospel. The name for each Sunday also follows the Revised Common Lectionary with other well-known names given in parentheses.

CONTENTS

Advent 1
Matthew 24: 36-44

Backwards for Christmas

*W*hy we have to start the year of Matthew with chapter 24 is a mystery, unless you are one of those readers who like to peek at the end of the story before deciding to start reading. Such underhanded readers understand that the end has a lot to tell us about how worthwhile the whole story will be.

We could have started with Matthew's genealogy this Advent, but that is probably too tame. Fourteen generations times three, ending with Joseph. Except that Joseph actually was not the father of our Lord. Fourteen times three generations rudely interrupted by four women who surely cannot be relevant to the final story. Except that any genealogist knows we can be more certain of the mother of a child than of the father. So Matthew is giving clues from the start that this story is unusual. Perhaps even in his day, there was a tendency to romanticize the story with angels mysteriously humming and cows gently lowing in squeaky-clean stables. Except that babies were slaughtered all around the stable.

Why is it so important to look to the end of Matthew? At important points in my life I have taken special note of the way we say goodbye. It has enlightened me about the evangelists taking so long over the last week of Jesus' life. The goodbyes sum up the worth of a relationship, a job, a life. The more worthwhile, the harder the goodbye.

But how worthwhile is this coming of the Son of Humanity? It will be like the days of Noah. Not that eating and drinking and marrying are bad things to be doing. Nor is working in a field or grinding meal. They are ordinary patterns of life. They are the expected, the normal, the everyday. But the Day of this Coming will sweep over us like the great flood of Noah. Chaos will destroy normality. It will be as if a thief has broken into your house.

From the beginning of his Gospel, Matthew describes an intrusive coming of strange and foreign women; a coming of fathers who are shaken to the core by their child who is not their child; a coming of kings with ghastly death shadowing their every step.

Matthew will detail for his readers the way the Hebrew scriptures have been fulfilled in the coming of Jesus, and I don't just refer to the iffy way we use Isaiah and the prophets around Christmas. In today's reading from the end of Matthew's story, we look right back to the creation stories, to the beginning, to the terrifying and destructive waters that covered the earth. It may be very sensible to peek at the ending, lest we find that this story is not for us. It may be that this inkling of the end will be too much for our polite religiosity.

Watch then! If God is coming, norms will be turned upside down. If you prefer your religion a little calmer than that, Matthew—from beginning to end—suggests you try another religion.

Advent 2
MATTHEW 3:1-12

🌿

If You Have Ears

I don't like people who bury their head in a book, or even worse in a sheet of paper, when the Gospel is announced in church. I much prefer the Gospel reading to be heard, though that of course depends on its being read well.

However, in my reading to prepare for today's passage, I couldn't help noticing what listeners would miss. John has just finished preaching his head off, metaphorically speaking, at this stage. He points to One who will come baptizing with fire, who will sort the wheat from the chaff. Then, in verse thirteen, we read that Jesus came to be baptized by John!

Was John the Baptist a little disappointed with this introduction to his cousin's formal ministry? Jesus came to be baptized and John *was* rather peeved. He questioned the wisdom of Jesus' request, and justifiably so. John had been preaching for a while; Jesus was just starting. Nevertheless John had more to learn, even from his own preaching.

Out there in the wilderness, where poetry flourishes, the Baptist had mixed his metaphors masterfully, and the people of Jerusalem and Judea came to hear, confess, and be washed. As the city emptied into the desert, the religious leaders, the priests and the teachers, also came to listen. And they were condemned, condemned for presuming that they were the sole owners of the truth from God. Ancestry, privileged position, even great scholarship, could not be presumed upon. The truth that sets us free is too wide for the fences we love to put around it. God's truth breaks my pathetic boundaries. May it always be so.

This is the hardest balancing act I find in preaching: how to speak with authority without acting as if I own the message, how to listen as I preach, how to preach to others and also allow the Word to preach to me. It bothers me that while the church tradition which gave birth to me proclaims the centrality of the Word of God it often sets more store by big-name preachers of the Word.

The Sadducees and Pharisees did not own God's truth, and John told them so in no uncertain terms. But when it came to putting God in a box, John found he also had a box. True, it was a Baptist-sized box, but it was still a box.

When Jesus follows our little efforts at preaching, we too can expect him to come in ways that shake our theology to its core. It is not that Jesus will mind too much that we argue with him about his way of proceeding. He is pretty patient. But we had better let him have it his way in the end or we may well miss hearing God's voice. We had better be willing to open our hands and let go of the Word of truth, lest we trim it down to a message that is not worth hearing.

Advent 3
MATTHEW 11:2-11
※

Out of Bounds

Well, that's it. I've done my best. I've preached my heart out. I've tried and tried to communicate. I admit there's something of the actor, the sensationalist in me, so I haven't been averse to dressing up the occasion, dressing up myself. But now, that's it. Herod's henchmen have got me where they want me. It's over.

The powers of this world, yes, and of the people of God, have all had their criticisms to make of me. Quite justifiably. After all I criticized them first. My motives have not been pure but let them cast the first stone if they have pure motives. I only want it remembered that I opened my mouth in the first place because I wanted desperately to speak the truth. I set my face towards the water, towards the chaos of the deep. I have not turned back from truth wherever it led me. I have suffered for the truth, but that's okay. I knew it would be so. My only regret is what I did not foresee, that I have been trampled in the crush, not the crush of God's truth rolling down like a stream, but the crush of those rushing away from the depths of truth. That is why my spirit is broken. Because they preferred half the truth and no truth at all.

I've done my best and I'm sorry if it was not good enough. I too repent of my sins and my inadequacies. I too need cleansing. And here you are, the new guy around town, preaching good news and the kingdom of God. You could carry on this work of truth-telling, but you are so different. Was I right when I said that you are the One? Do you love the truth as much as I do? You love the towns and cities a little too much for my liking.

Me, I loved the desert. They called me crazy for living out there. I loved the dry dust and rocky ground, the crusty wadis that speak of past and future roaring water. But you, you seem to revel in civilization, in towns and cities. I am relieved to hear that you occasionally head off into the wild places for prayer and peace.

You hear the town gossip so you must know I am in prison. Prisons are part of cities and civilization. No prisons out there in the desert, in my beautiful wilderness. Prisons are civilized. The civilized ones don't like crazy people like me coming to tell them they need liberating. So they try to civilize me by putting me in their prison. They think they will chop off my rough edges by putting me in this little box. Well, they will have to chop off my head, for that's where the roughest edge is.

But still I can't help wondering if I was mistaken. What if you are not the One? Will you come along the path I have made for you in the desert or will you prefer the cities, the civilization, the organization, the control, the safe and predictable things of this age? I warn you, if you follow the truth that I preached you will be despised and rejected by the civilized. In the end you will be consumed by the uncivilized truth.

Advent 4
MATTHEW 1:18-25

Dream, Dream, Dream

Small children who have no sense of a historical timeline tend to confuse the Joseph in this story with the Joseph in Genesis. Reading Matthew's story, we could pardon their error. If the Christmas cards are anything to go by, this later Joseph also had a coat with long sleeves and many colors. But, more importantly, this Joseph was also a dreamer.

He dreamt of the angel of the Lord who told this righteous Joseph not to be afraid and, in effect, to do "the wrong thing." Joseph dreamt and was told to run away to the place of slavery and salvation of his namesake, to Egypt. He dreamt and was told to return to Israel. He dreamt a warning and decided to go to tiny Nazareth in the Galilee instead of Judea. If Stephen were to preach this story as he exegeted the Old Testament salvation history in the Acts of the Apostles, he might be stoned to death again. Especially when you realize that the other main characters in this plot who also dream warnings are a bunch of New-Agers out of the east. It is not quite pukka Israelite.

But we only need to glance at the strange women who appear in Matthew's genealogy to see that righteousness in God's sight is not always what it seems in human eyes. The women of Matthew chapter one are women on the edge of Israel who live in sexually doubtful situations. They survive, even flourish, by their assertiveness, by working the system. Tamar had to prostitute herself to produce righteousness in the man who finally gave her rightful children by marriage. Rahab was a prostitute, a woman living on the fringe even of Canaanite society, who bought life for the future leader of God's people by her cunning and quick wit. Ruth, the Moabite, risked a fate worse than death to wake up God's people to care for the widows and orphans in their midst as their God had clearly commanded. The wife of Uriah, perhaps a Hittite herself, was abused by the leader of God's people and yet brought forth the wisdom of Israel. These women, by hook or by crook, opened the way for God's promise to be fulfilled.

When it came to yet another woman in a sexually unusual and vulnerable situation*, naturally this righteous Joseph needed encouragement to do the wrong thing. He was told to do the wrong thing so that the scriptures might be fulfilled, so that God might be with us. Dare we ask the question: What if Joseph had done the right thing?

Perhaps Tertullian had it rather wrong. It is not so much the martyrs but the heretics who are the lifeblood of the church. How many righteous among God's own people do not dare to dream? How many good believers live only out of their fearful adherence to law and do not heed the angel of the Lord? How many people of excellent genealogy hesitate and finally miss seeing Emmanuel, God-with-us?

May the last days that the prophets foretold be ever with us. May the young continue to see visions and the old to dream dreams.

*See Francis J. Moloney, *Woman First Among the Faithful: A New Testament Study,* Dove Communications, Blackburn, Victoria, 1984, 36.

Christmas Day
LUKE 2:1-20

🎄

Laughter in Heaven

I have heard preachers who distinguish joy from mere happiness. Joy is not something, they would say, that is as superficial as laughter. But me, well, I would be glad some days for a bit of mere superficial laughter.

There are different sorts of laughter. There is laughing *with* someone and laughing *at* someone. There is an embarrassed giggle and a full belly laugh. After a year in which I was called to take more funerals than usual, my local funeral director had the good idea of holding seminars to help people cope with Christmas which is meant to be such a happy time, but which for many brings a raw memory of tragedy. What struck me was that those who were even a little in touch with their emotions wept unashamedly. But they also laughed in the next breath unashamedly when recalling good or funny things about the person they had lost.

It seems that there is something healthy, something healing, that happens when the tears and laughter get mixed up like that. It is not so much that there are tears that give way to laughter but that sadness and joy are not far from each other.

Take Sarah for instance. Sarah laughed when told that she would have a son. She was too old. It was impossible. It was, I suppose, a laugh that was bitter, a cynical laugh. But when Isaac was born he was called

Laughter in honor of her merriment, which was now real joy, and real enough not to take any notice of the boring theology that says joy is somehow above laughter.

The content of God's promise to Sarah and Abraham, when the whole world was caught in the avalanche of sin and stupidity that even the great flood hadn't sorted out, the content of the promise to bless all nations through this one childless couple, consisted of the creation of something out of nothing, life out of death. The content was one child, called Laughter. The content of God's promise was in fact one huge belly laugh. And the content of God's promise is still one big belly laugh.

I heard a journalist asking South Africans how they felt after six months of government by Mandela. Desmond Tutu simply replied "Yippee!" That's how he felt and that's how he feels. He has gotten in touch with the great belly laugh at the center of the universe.

Desmond Tutu is the only man I can think of who could have made such a fool of himself, jumping up and down, not at all like a bishop should act, shouting yippee like a comic strip character, lost in the laughter, completely without dignity in the foolishness of it all. Because Desmond Tutu understands, he knows, he feels the great cosmic joke.

Even the angels can't contain their laughter at the end of this Gospel reading. Our bible translation makes it sound very religious, praising God, but it is the "suddenly" that gives it away. It burbles up in them and threatens to engulf the entire universe.

One child, a child of a woman who can't possibly be pregnant, one child, laughing Boy, the content of God's promise, to bring good out of evil, life out of death, creation out of nothing, laughter out of tears.

The Laughter did come, the Laughter is coming, the Laughter will come again.

ISAAC

Funny fellow, Isaac.
What's God see in you?

Mother laughed behind God's back
Stirring Mamre stew.

But her barrenness was past.
Sneers turned into joy.
Sarah saw the joke at last.
Called him "Laughing-boy." *

Laughter can be kind or cruel.
Ishmael at play
Made the Laughing-boy a fool.
He was sent away.

Trudging up Moriah's hill
Knife in father's hand,
Were you quick to do his will
Or slow to understand?
Where's the lamb for sacrifice?
Finally you sighed.
Killing children isn't nice.
(Though God's own son died!)

Not a single decent tale
That's not been told before.
Isaac, coward, foolish, frail,
And worst of all, a bore!

Laughing-boy, God's huge joke,
What's to see in you?
Blessing boring foolish folk,
God will bless me too!

*Thanks to John Goldingay for the translation of Isaac as "Laughing-boy."

Christmas 1
(Also known as Holy Family)
MATTHEW 2:13-23

Wrestling with the Word

*P*art of the curious friendship that has developed between me and the text of scripture is that we are not afraid to argue with each other. Good doctrine tells me that I ought to submit to the text's agenda, to let it ask its questions of me, to really listen, to only listen. So occasionally I have been silent and waited for the text to address me.

At precisely those times I have found my friend saying to me, "Would you read this and tell me what you think. Is it unclear? Incomplete? Don't be afraid to be critical." So I, who would find it simpler to treat the text like God, am encouraged to read critically. And as the text and I take each other seriously, a conversation is set up. A friendship grows that bridges the great gulf of time and space and language. It happens because we respect each other's humanity.

My friend, I have a few criticisms today. I liked where Matthew began, that marvelous genealogy with its strong women. But it took you a mere seventeen verses to launch into a Christmas story in which the Virgin is completely silenced while Joseph churns into action. Is this what is meant by God-with-us, that men act while women follow serenely? Thank God Luke tells a slightly different tale. Or are you trying to tell me something more by putting Matthew and Luke together in the same scriptures?

This role for women was mirrored in the set of readings provided by the Three Year Lectionary for the Sunday after Christmas entitled "The family." It began with both male and female created in God's image (Genesis 1), moved easily into the wife as the fruitful vine of her husband (Psalm 128), thence to a letter of Paul which tells wives to submit to their husbands (Colossians 3). By the time we reached Matthew, Joseph was busy packing the station wagon: "Come on, dear, off to Egypt today" and "Nazareth looks nice." Mary quietly makes the sandwiches and fills the thermos.

I also have my suspicions about your exegetical methods. I assume that you have done your homework on the prophets, but on the surface it looks like mere word association: Egypt, son, children, weeping, Nazorean, Nazareth. It is a little unclear and I don't want you to give the wrong idea to those who don't realize your expert knowledge of the Hebrew scriptures. Some of them may not be rude enough to answer back.

You did ask for my opinion, remember. Today I am feeling there really is half a world between us, and how distant we are, you and I.

My biggest criticism I leave until last. It may not be a criticism of you as such. I may have to go to a higher court with this one. Do you realize the impression you've given about the children slaughtered at Bethlehem? This is not good public relations for God when the beloved son is whisked away to safety while others are killed in his place. What sort of God is this you present to us? It was meant to be the other way around.

Christmas 2
JOHN 1:1-18
(Alternate: Epiphany—Matthew 2:1-12;
see following section)
🌱

Flesh and Grace

*T*he Word became flesh but we did not believe. You can't blame us really for not believing. It is rather ridiculous to say that the Word became flesh. We have been trying to hide it ever since it was first said. We still pretend not to believe the words of the Creed about the resurrection of the body. We sing sweet songs at Christmas about a little baby, rejoicing in the Incarnation but we don't really like our own bodies, even though God took our flesh.

One of the big questions that came out of the women's ordination debate for me was whether Christ took on my flesh, for "what was not assumed was not saved."* If male and female flesh are so very different, if, as some practically suggested, God really is a boy's name, then Christ is hardly able to be my savior. I am not for one moment suggesting that Jesus was not a male human being, but the emphasis for the theology of the Incarnation is that he was a human being. The maleness was, if you like, a scandal of particularity.

The only argument that held any water for me in that difficult time came from a friend who suggested that to ordain women as priests would be to mess around with "the poetry of it all." As one who appreciates poetry, I could almost have been convinced by the argument. But most others insisted on arguing from sloppy exegesis or ecclesiology rather than poetry, so I stuck to my guns. There might be something about the Son of the Father being born of a Woman. But as soon as we try to figure out what the something is, the theology leaks badly.

Whatever the status of the poetry, I reckoned that if Christ died for me it had to be at least conceivable that the second person of the Trinity could take on female flesh. However, when I voiced this idea one Advent before some learned theologians, I had to retract it very quickly, for one of them went red in the face and looked set for a heart attack. The unlikely conception simply ended up in another poem for Christmas:

ANOTHER CHRISTMAS

It ought to be conceivable (but can a man conceive?)
That God once came in female flesh, and no one would believe;
That she gave birth and spent her life of three score years and ten
In giving very flesh and blood for building up of men;
That somehow, graciously, from God, the true Maidservant came
And washed our feet with salty tears. And we forgot her name!
Or that she gave the smallest hint that here was something more
Beyond an earthly intercourse, and so was called a whore;
Or told her story openly, and, for her children's sake,
Refused to take the story back, and suffered at the stake.
In other words, if God-with-us just did what women do,
Would we have simply passed her by or crucified her too?

*Gregory Nazianzus, Epistle 101, *Christology of the Later Fathers,* ed. E.R.Hardy, SCM, 1954, 218.

Epiphany
MATTHEW 2:1-12

The Little People

They may have been kings but this text does not actually say so. There were not necessarily three of them either, which only goes to show how much hymns and songs influence our theological interpretations. We can guess that they must have had some financial resources to have made such a long journey, though the camels may be a mere figment of the imagination of Christmas card manufacturers.

One pensioner who comes to our church for regular food parcels lives in a sub standard hostel where the electricity and heating are turned off at five am. He always keeps himself looking immaculate no matter how early he has to rise for a shower. In midwinter he keeps warm by buying an all-day ticket and riding the trains. He is always wearing a coat and tie and is a politely spoken gentleman. You could almost be mistaken for thinking he comes from an upper-class suburb. Well, were the three wise men rich or poor, upper or lower class, important politicians or well-dressed nobodies?

We must admit that picture of a second bunch of little people turning up at Bethlehem after the shepherds does not suit the poetry and drama of our Christmas pageants. These men must have had some presence born of royalty to have the audacity to go straight to the top, to King

Herod, with their queries. However, the text says that they did not go straight to Herod. Herod sent for them after being worried by their brazen questions out in the highways and byways. Then "he sent them to Bethlehem" to do his dirty work for him.

They were said to be the magi, the wise ones, and knowledge may be bought with gold, but wisdom has a higher price. Ah, yes, we see, they had treasure chests and gold and other odd items from the New Age shop which they produced as gifts for the child. Another of my pensioner friends occasionally produces items of jewelry which "fell off the back of a truck," which he is willing to give away for a song, even to the church.

I thus puzzle over the economic status of these fellows because I see that their story is part of a wondrous minority story. Bethlehem, in the land of Judea, despite the sloppy translation of Micah's prophetic words by Herod's scribes, was the least of towns. Kings should be born in Jerusalem, or at least in another of Herod's palaces throughout the land. Perhaps the royal scribes could not bear to translate a text which suggested such an important matter happening in such a second-rate town.

That Herod the Great had not even heard of the birth of a new king filled him with fear, for he was losing control of his monopoly of power.* The people of Jerusalem were also frightened. All that they had ever known prepared them for power residing where it always had, at the top. How dare the prophet say that the little village down the road, outside the walls, was the birthplace of the Messiah! It just goes to prove what a little prophet Micah really was.

The words of true prophets are anathema to the government whose business is to keep everyone in their proper estate: the rich man in his castle, the poor man at his gate, God "made them all bright and beautiful" and ordered. But suddenly three outsiders arrive in town and they turn everything upside down.

---

*See Walter Brueggemann, *Interpretation and Obedience: From Faithful Reading to Faithful Living,* Fortress Press, Minneapolis, 1991, 273.

Baptism of the Lord
(Ordinary Sunday 1)
MATTHEW 3:13-17

Prevent us, O Lord

It is a difficult time for those who have the task of writing our modern prayer books. The language needs to be accessible enough for human beings without being too vulgar to utter before God, mysterious enough to enable worship of almighty God without being totally incomprehensible to humans. On the other hand, the God of Jesus seemed content enough with everyday Greek for the recording of his second set of scriptures. We should not be too lofty in our language spoken towards God.

I am old enough to have a soft spot for the old Anglican Book of Common Prayer. I like its rhythms and its language that doesn't give away all its secrets in one rush. I remember the deep sense of satisfaction I felt as a teenager, having recently come to faith, and joined the Church of England in Australia, and beginning to understand the language of our prayer book. I don't think it was mere pride that I felt when my Latin lessons enabled me to see that the beautiful prayer "Prevent us, O Lord, in all our doings" was not about stopping us from doing something but about going before us. It was for me a time of entering into an ancient faith that only gradually gave up its secrets.

The prayer books may have changed but the faith is still both incredibly old and forever fresh.

John the Baptist prevented Jesus in the ancient sense and would have prevented him in the modern sense as well, except that Jesus insisted on baptism. St John is the only other evangelist who notices the problem. Only Matthew attempts to explain the odd situation, and it becomes for him a matter of righteousness fulfilled.

The words from heaven that follow the baptism, according to Matthew, are an announcement to those present rather than to Jesus: "This is my beloved." So also St John could testify that he saw and heard the opening of heaven that was taking place. Jesus enters the waters of a baptism of repentance, but what we have here is more than a mere example of humility. Jesus enters our world and fills it to overflowing.

Not only do we still need the Lord to prevent us but also to fulfill us in our worship, not only with our lips but in our lives. We only dare to pray because Jesus has gone before us. Through his death he has opened up the heavens to our cries and, never one to leave a job half finished, he prayed on our behalf and taught us words to pray. The Spirit of Jesus continues to come upon his followers and fill our empty words and unutterable groans with meaning.

"Prevent us, O Lord, in all our doings with thy most gracious favor, and further us with thy continual help; that in all our works begun, continued, and ended in thee, we may glorify thy holy Name, and finally by thy mercy obtain everlasting life; through Jesus Christ our Lord. Amen."

Epiphany 2
(Ordinary Sunday 2)
JOHN 1:29-42

Abide with Me

John the Baptist testified about Jesus that he was, and is and will be, the Lamb of God, the one who baptizes with the Holy Spirit, the Son of God. It was John's very purpose in life to testify to the light, so that all might believe. It is the purpose of the one who writes this story. It is our ministry too, to testify and step aside.

There is no indication that John the Baptist's first testimony had an audience. It may be that the baptism also was a more private affair than good sacramental theologians would like. Whether or not these verses were John's first private theological musings, he was certainly stretching the boundaries of the Hebrew scriptures by aligning the paschal lamb with the sin of the whole world, a unique relationship with the Father and the Spirit with sacrifice and suffering. Setting his musings alongside his experience of the coming of the Spirit in the baptism of Jesus, John feels confident enough to give a more public pronouncement the following day: "Look, here is the Lamb of God." The Spirit's descending on and dwelling with this man Jesus has convinced John that Jesus is the promised one, the fulfillment of John's ministry, the object of his testimony.

From this moment it is over to Jesus. But, strangely, on this the first official day of the ministry of Jesus, the man himself says and does very little. His very presence on the scene by itself seems to shift quite enough in the universe for one day's work. John's testimony has caused two disciples to transfer their allegiance. Jesus has asked one question about the intentions of these two and then, seemingly satisfied with their odd answer, has invited them to inspect the goods. They begin their association by calling Jesus "Rabbi." By the end of the day they claim to have found the Messiah.

Does one day spent in the place where Jesus is staying prove so much to enquiring minds? Yet to know where Jesus was staying was their first desire, precisely their reply to his query about their intentions. *Where, indeed, was he staying?*

The storyteller has informed us that the Word dwelt in the beginning with God and that God's Son dwells close to the Father's heart. The Baptist has seen Jesus as the dwelling place of God's Spirit. One day standing at the threshold of the dwelling place of this man from Nazareth is surely worth a thousand days spent dwelling in the tents of the ungodly. One day discovering where Jesus was staying was enough for Andrew to search out his brother and bring him under the light of Jesus' gaze.

It is desperately sad to be informed by the writer that the Word made flesh came to dwell with his own people and was rejected.

Epiphany 3
(Ordinary Sunday 3)
MATTHEW 4:12-23

Going Places

*E*veryone associated with this story seems destined to go places. Jesus himself was born to travelers, his first visitors came from distant lands to find him, his first international trip to Egypt was at a young age, and now he has made a smaller but no less significant transfer from Nazareth to Capernaum by the Sea of Galilee to begin his public ministry.

It is through geography that Matthew often makes his associations with the Hebrew scriptures and it is the lands of the gentiles that feature most often, from the women of Matthew's genealogy to this latest movement of Jesus which introduces the call of his first disciples. Simon Peter, Andrew, James and John can only expect that, if they follow Jesus, their travels will lead them away from home into uncharted waters, into foreign territory.

If you would leave your fishing and father to follow Jesus, be aware, right from the outset, that there is nothing safe about discipleship.

The lands of Zebulun and Naphtali had suffered under invading armies, most notably the unbelievably vicious Assyrians, because these territories were on the main trade route, the international highway to power and fortune. The lush and fertile lands of Galilee mask the pain of history that is only just below the surface, but be assured that the stones here also continue to cry out.

Naphtali, of the northernmost of the tribes, "lived among the Canaanites" (Judges 1:33) and was particularly vulnerable. It was pretty much always gentile territory. It was despised by Jerusalem because of its northern location and because its population was the first to be deported by the feared Tiglathpileser.

Zebulun was also the homeland of Jonah, and Jesus will shortly stand in this territory by the sea, debating with the Pharisees and delivering to them the great sign of Jonah in the belly of the sea monster.

On the other hand, this territory of Zebulun and Naphtali was precisely the place where Isaiah prophesied that a great light would shine. This place that was most vulnerable, most utterly destroyed, most trampled over, most invaded by armies and ideas, was the place that God would make his homebase to preach the kingdom of heaven.

On reflection, this pain-filled land is the place God is most likely to choose. Furthermore, the prophet Jonah, we may now reflect, was destined to travel far and wide with good news whether he liked it or not.

Epiphany 4
(Ordinary Sunday 4)
MATTHEW 5:1-12

Some people think it is a rather crass rendering of the Beatitudes to say: "Happy are...." It probably reminds them of those awful posters that trivialized happiness into things like a warm puppy! But the blessings found here are tangible and earthy enough to make me argue for a translation which is comprehensible to ordinary human beings who do not share my religious vocabulary. Jesus promises happiness for those who are just plain unhappy now. More than that, Jesus announces that happiness is not merely future but now.

I have a friend who often asks what happiness is. I confess I don't have too many answers for her. She loves Jesus, deeply. She loves her neighbor, with her time and money, not just words. But she happens to be caught between two cultures, and between two families, a natural family and a foster family, and in the end she feels as if she belongs to neither. Paradoxically, when I spend time with her, I end up feeling deeply happy, so I worry that she does not know what happiness is. For my friend, words like blessedness and joy are too highfalutin. She would be pleased with just a little happiness in her life. Except she doesn't know what it is.

I asked a friend who was dying what would make him really happy. He said, "I wish I had learned to drive a car." We worked out that it was not the car he wanted, or the driving lessons, it was the freedom. He admitted he would really prefer a bicycle ride.

"Alone?" I asked. He remembered rides when he was younger and healthier with one good friend. It was the feel of wind on their faces, the freedom and the friendship that really mattered. It was also the sense of going somewhere, of traveling. Not that the destination mattered greatly, but that there was a destination that gave meaning to the journey.

Another friend tells the story of a vacation when she stopped her car to get out and go along a trail looking for a site that was meant to be a special tourist attraction. The signpost said it was a few yards down the track. She walked and walked, allowing some margin for error. She enjoyed the scenery, but she never did find the tourist attraction and finally went back to her car bemused. She assumes she passed the site in her wanderings, but never recognized it. Nevertheless she admitted that the walk itself had been delightful and she is not at all sorry she had taken the path.

The word "blessed" of course does help us to compare and contrast these sayings with other biblical blessings, with older blessings which had conditions attached, with pilgrims arriving at the temple of God, with the Aaronic blessing which associates blessing with God's grace and peace, and most beautifully with the face of God.

Jesus' new disciples had had an exciting initiation: preaching, healing, exorcisms, and huge crowds. After this first frantic tour of duty they went up the hill to find Jesus and they sat with him. With God's face turned to them, they were blessed. No conditions attached. They were happy.

Epiphany 5
(Ordinary Sunday 5)
MATTHEW 5:13-20

❧

Don't Look Back

Salt in the scriptures is a strange commodity and I don't know enough about chemical formulae or the Hebrew language to work out if it is the same commodity we are talking about all the way through. If an army wanted to reduce its victims to complete despair, they could salt the fields and render the land infertile. On the other hand, Elisha used salt to sweeten the bad waters of Jericho. It was, presumably, the preservative properties of salt that sealed the covenant of God with the people. I notice that an industry is thriving around the Dead Sea and its minerals today, but I don't know what theological point to make of that. What Jesus had in mind when he mentioned salt is not immediately certain. Anyway, in this passage he speaks more about a lack of saltiness and a light foolishly hidden from view, salt that is not salt and light that is not light.

It was in a moment of despair that Lot's wife came sweetly into my view, so that I heard her speak, heard her communication, even in her salty paralysis. To this day she is preserved still, looking over her shoulder at the past and the what-ifs. Odd that her daughters excused their subsequent incestuous behavior as a preservative measure.

I suspect that women do a lot of looking back. They look back to the past with regret and render themselves unable to get on with life. They can become completely paralysed, like Lot's wife. In those six long years I had to wait between the deaconing and the priesting of women in my church, I spent many hours just sitting and pondering. Someone once suggested I move to another country where women were being priested, but I couldn't even begin to think of such a move. Were they wasted years, I wonder?

And so Lot's wife revealed herself to me. Her only fault the backward glance. A pillar of salt. And Jesus said we are to be like salt! You can't really let go of the past until you have looked back and looked deeply at what has gone before. After all, Lot's daughters and Lot himself may have escaped the fate of Sodom and of salt, but their subsequent actions show they were hardly freed from Sodom's influence. Perhaps we can only be what we can be.

LOT'S WIFE
"Don't look back!" the warning came. Which only goes to prove
that this is very much the world of men in which we move,
for women live by looking back, connecting now and then,
unable to dislodge the past and simply start again.
Women dine on past events. They savor every crumb
to feed the soul, replenish strength, and face what is to come:
past people and relationships, including Sodom's years.
So you were caught by blinding light. Or blinded by your tears.
And now you stand, forever salt, distilled from every tear.
Your only fault, the backward glance. Alternative: unclear.
And generations after you were pilloried; who'd guess
another One would speak of light, and value saltiness.

The Law of Life

*T*his passage from the Sermon on the Mount raises the question of the relationship between the first and second testaments. One wonders how Marcion and his pals managed to ignore Jesus' warning given here that he was on about fulfillment, not abolition of the old. I suppose Marcion decided that this part of scripture could be ignored because it did not fit his preconceived ideas.

I haven't quite given in to Marcion's heresy, but I do find myself rather uneasy in the presence of such a text, because I too have preconceived ideas. I prefer my Gospel in terms of grace rather than law. If I must err one way or the other, I admit it will probably be to cheapen grace rather than to allow works any kind of foothold. And here Jesus seems to be making the old laws not more grace-full, but simply harder to keep than ever before. "You've heard talk about laws but you ain't heard nothing yet."

I also happen to love the Old Testament. It gives a breadth to faith that the New Testament, because of its decisive subject matter and because it was written over a shorter timespan, can never have. But I am not sure what to do with all those laws. The distinction between ceremonial and moral laws is over simplified. Who decides which is ceremonial, and passing, and which is moral, and therefore relevant? Anyway, the Old Testament never seems to divide its laws in quite that way.

Ah, but we read the Old Testament with New Testament eyes, you say. The New Testament is our real scripture, the fulfillment of the Old. And with proof texts about old and new wineskins we side with Marcion rather more than we ought. Against such views, John Goldingay suggests that "the question was not whether the Old Testament was Christian but whether the New Testament was biblical." *

In today's passage Jesus speaks of the new fulfilling the old, but fulfillment does not mean that the old law is superseded or finished with. Rather it is filled out or, to mix metaphors, brought into sharper focus. Now that Jesus is with us, we are not to be concerned so much with keeping the letter of the law but with an impossible spirit of the law. Not only is murder anti-law, so is anger. Not only adultery, but lust. Let's face it, Jesus said divorce is adultery. Jesus' exegesis invites us to continue exegeting the myriad other parts of the old law we know to be life-giving.

The law was given as a gift to God's people, a way of life which built up community, which produced shalom. We, with all who love to turn grace into works, prefer to think in terms of laws, "oughts" and "should nots." Jesus does not, cannot abolish this law, this life-giving gift. He fills it full. For those who turn law into laws, it sounds as if there are simply more things to do wrong. The promise that Jesus preaches is of God's law given for our well-being and bringing a life fuller than we can imagine.

Approaches to Old Testament Interpretation, Apollos, Leicester, updated edition, 1990, 34.

Epiphany 7
(Ordinary Sunday 7)
MATTHEW 5:38-48

Doormat Theology

No sensible schoolteacher tells a child simply to turn the other cheek to a bully. That is an invitation to become a doormat, used and abused by others who are trying to stake out territory. Good teachers give the child ways of understanding their own behavior and feelings. They give victims defensive techniques, ways of asserting themselves against bullies. Then, of course, they go and do something about the bullies who find it so necessary to bash others.

I seem to remember a Peanuts cartoon—and if I remember wrongly, it is still in line with the creator's general theology—in which Charlie Brown turns the other cheek and is belted a second time for his trouble. Charlie looks quizzical. It wasn't meant to be like that. Weren't there meant to be coals of fire heaped on the enemy's head somewhere in all this? The enemy was meant to repent or at least be shamed into submission. But let's face it, Charlie Brown's fate is the more likely. History bears us out that such passive resistance will be rewarded with immediate anger. Such generosity and love will breed resentment. We are not only likely to be struck on the other cheek, but to have our throat cut as well.

Gandhi and Martin Luther King Jr had their faults, even their failures, but they grasped the power of this odd way of living in our world. They would tell Charlie Brown that he ought not to be so naive as to look puzzled when the left cheek is struck, when there is no item of clothing left to keep out the cold, when the second backpacking mile and the third and the fourth come round. Charlie must realize that turning the other cheek, refusing to save oneself or one's community, is an ethical and political decision with mind-boggling ramifications.

Jesus has been teaching about the filling out of God's law. Like a good rabbi, he provides his disciples with a little case study concerning the law. But ever so subtly in the process he has been deconstructing the whole idea of the law with its justice and fairness, its protection of the community and the individual.

This is the rabbi of whom it was said, "We never heard anyone teach like this." This is the rabbi who teaches God's law like the new thing it was always meant to be. This is the rabbi who talks more like a prophet. He opens up possibilities for alternative ways of living with what the Roman occupation forces assume is the only way to live. There is food for thought here for the proponents of social justice. But more than this, the rabbi opens up possibilities of living within the community of God's chosen people which tends to domesticate the word that is meant to bring new life.

Let me tell you, Charlie Brown, whoever follows these instructions will be walked over. No doubt about it. This is doormat theology at its best. But doormats are not merely decorative. As they pick up the grime and mud of the world's feet, they become the foundation of a whole new way of living.

Epiphany 8
(Ordinary Sunday 8)
MATTHEW 6:24-34

An Age of Anxiety

The recession seemed to take longer to catch on in the church than in the rest of society. But it certainly made it in the end. There are fewer people putting money in the collection plate, and less money to be put in the plate; these are people who are incredibly overworked because they are trying to hold onto their jobs, people who are incredibly exhausted and depressed who can't find a job. The anxiety does not bypass the clergy. A few years ago I knew many schoolteachers who were unhappy in their present positions, but afraid to move lest they lose their job altogether. I suspect the clergy are now facing similar fears, with no easy answers except redundancy packages. And then whatever happened to a lifetime vocation to ministry?

There are many small congregations making ends meet with second-hand shops and building rentals or part-time clergy. People are asking their clergy to be accountable and parish councils are considering how to run their church like a business. On the other hand, people are often looking for intimacy at church in an age of fast food chains and multinational companies, so there are pressures to keep churches too small to survive. All this makes for a lot of anxious people and I would guess that there is more dissatisfaction between ministers and people than ever before.

At an international level, we are more aware of our destructive tendencies as a human race towards each other and the earth we live on. It makes the words of Jesus hard to swallow. It may be that within a few years there will be no flowers or birds left to compare with Solomon in all his glory.

However, Walter Brueggemann wisely points out that "such anxiety is not lodged among the have-nots, but among those who have."* The people who really worry me in these difficult times are not those who have always been at the bottom of the scale. The ones I know are pretty wily and know their way around the welfare agencies. I tremble more for the young middle-class kids who may never know what it is like to have a job, although we have kept them at school on the basis of a myth that says they will get a job if they get a good education. I worry about the middle-aged fathers who pretend to go to work each day because they are too scared to tell their family that they lost their job.

This scripture is even more important in such a time for such a people. It is high time we learnt that we are not self-sufficient, we are not self-made, and that to have once thought we were was only ever an illusion. We are not any more secure than sparrows whose life is in God's hand. When you think about it, that is not such an insecure place to be. How much life can we hold in our hand, can we gather into our barn, even if we are anxious all our years? Only a drop in the ocean compared with the life given by God each day.

* *Finally Comes the Poet: Daring Speech for Proclamation*, Fortress Press, Minneapolis, 1989, 94.

Epiphany Last:
Transfiguration
MATTHEW 17:1-9
(Not included in some lectionaries; also the
alternate reading for Lent 2)

Something Really Scary

Do you remember the scene in *Twilight Zone: the Movie* where Dan Ackroyd says to his companion in the car, "You want to see something really scary?" He rips off his everyday face to reveal a nasty ghoul, frightens the life out of his companion, and thereby sets the tone for the rest of the movie where things aren't always what they seem. But I remember the scariest thing about that movie was knowing that some actors had actually died in the making of it when a helicopter fell on them. I remember being pleasantly scared myself by the special effects and using the pause button on the video machine to show some young friends that it was not as scary as it seemed. I remember also taking a positively ghoulish pleasure in trying to identify where they'd had to cut a scene to cover the loss of a major character.

In Matthew's transfiguration scene we have a cut to the real world. Yes, the real world. This is how it really is underneath the nice picture of a wandering rabbi who teaches pleasant things. The transfiguration is a kind of cutting room ploy to make up for the sudden prediction of the loss of a major character from the plot.

Matthew's story of this moment on the mountain seems rather more deliberate than the one told by other Gospel writers. There are reminders of Moses on a mountain with a shining face and the shining cloud. The voice from the cloud can be identified precisely with the voice heard at Jesus' baptism. Even Matthew's disciples seem less foolish in their responses to what they have seen and heard. There are hints of the risen Lord raising his disciples to new life. So Matthew works this cameo skillfully into his story, with sermons sprouting out of every hint he gives.

Let's use the pause button and ask what actually happened on that mountain. "Come on, Peter, tell us."

"Well, we saw Jesus..."

"We disciples all see Jesus..."

"But this was different. He was shining."

"Nice lighting. What else?"

"Moses and Elijah were there."

"How did you know it was Moses and Elijah?"

"Can't explain it. We just did. There was a cloud and a voice..."

"Oh, we heard about that with John the Baptist at the Jordan river. What else?"

"We were really scared."

It is not all sweetness and balm to see things as they really are, even with the spotlights full on. Nor is it as simple as *Twilight Zone* made it seem. In their stripping away of the masks, the moviemakers did not go quite far enough. Want to see something really scary? Keep stripping.

I once heard some Christians explain their need for an exorcist after a particularly scary experience of a huge unknown presence trying to take over their lives. It may not have been pastorally sensitive of me, but I couldn't help asking, "How did you know it wasn't God?"

Lent 1
MATTHEW 4:1-11

And the Rest

*I*t's a funny kind of Gospel story. An incredibly private moment for Jesus of Nazareth before he gets into the swing of his Galilean ministry. Here's a question for you. If we are the body of Christ, as we like to say most Sundays, what does it mean that the body of Christ went into the wilderness, and what does this mean for us at Lent?

Matthew has enough hints that this Jesus is a kind of new Moses, so we should at least look back to the time of the forty years after Egypt. Jesus quotes a lot from Deuteronomy, the "second law" that is ascribed to Moses as a farewell speech as he has come so near and yet so far to the fulfillment of the promise.

Out in the wild places the tempter suggests to this new Moses that he do just the sort of thing that the first Moses did in the wilderness. Water from rock, bread from stones. What's the difference? This Jesus also stands on a mountain to view the promised land, except that there is a subtle and tempting twist about the content of the promise. Was it the same with Moses and the people of Israel?

Moses did something in the wilderness that I have never been quite able to put my theological finger on. He displeased God so much he was not allowed to enter the land beyond the Jordan. The only good I have ever found coming from that turn of events is that it led the writer to the Hebrews to write one of my favorite verses of scripture: "There remains still a rest for the people of God."

This Jesus did nothing to displease God. We know already that God was well pleased with him. Yet he rested in the grave three days and those three days were an eternity. I can't make theological sense of how those three days even existed.

What does it mean that the body of Christ goes into the wilderness? To walk again where Moses and the people of Israel walked, knowing the hunger and thirst of the desert before promises are fullfilled. That is what being the body means. To live again the journey which is interpreted and thus becomes another giving of the law of God. To know the gut-level meaning of the scriptures and to overcome the misuse that others will make even of God's word. That is what is meant by the church's preaching. To ponder our ministry and purpose in the world, not just as individuals, but as a community, and not to give in to easy answers, even if they sound on the surface godly answers about the definition of "church." To crave again the manna and quail that speak of grace and sabbath rest, but to know that the rest is still only seen in glimpses and remains to be seen in its fullness. That is what it means to venture into the season of Lent.

The other affirmation we make at worship is that the Spirit is with us. That presence will make all the difference to our glimpsing, our craving, our pondering, our preaching, our knowing. The rest is not yet. It remains still. But we know it is.

Lent 2
JOHN 3:1-17
(For lectionaries using Matthew 17:1-9, see Epiphany Last: Transfiguration, pp. 45)

Theology by Night

D o you remember the Christian camps we used to go to, when we got into the deepest and best theological discussions around midnight on Saturday just as the leaders wanted us to go to bed? Saturday night was usually concert night too, but they often put on a serious talk, or at least a Question and Answer forum. I always put in the question, anonymously of course, "How do you know when you are in love?" After five or six camps, I already knew the answer was, "You just know." But it was good for a giggle and it kept the camp parents on their toes.

One of the most responsible camp leaders I ever knew would schedule the serious talk with a stirring call to accept Christ early in the evening, but then follow straight on with the concert. If anyone wanted to go further with the Christ he preached, they had to wait till the laughter had died down. He wanted no one merely moved by the moment. It worked well, though it meant he was often left talking late into the night.

We should note that it was Nicodemus, the local theologian, who came to Jesus one night. Jesus told this theologian before all other people, "You must be born again." There is a deep simplicity about John 3:16 which suggests that all Christians are theologians and that we all need to be born again. This new birth is for insiders, not outsiders.

Nicodemus comes by night, and perhaps that gives him confidence to tell what he knows of Jesus and to further explore the truly deep things. He knows already that Jesus is a teacher from God. It is not the deepest insight in the world, but it is enough for the new rabbi to work with. What really matters is that such theologians bring their curiosity and theologizing to Jesus.

Some time after my mother died, I had a dream. I was lying in bed in a tight fetal position. A voice said, "You must be born again," and I knew I had to leave my mother behind and get on with life. It was a little frightening, but also normal and necessary. Staying too long in the womb is just another way to die. Even in middle age we theologians find the need to be born again, to stretch and breathe in the life of a strange new world.

One of my favorite quotes says: "Theological truths are discovered by open minds passionately hungry for contemporary, true understanding of God." * But such truth is not mere camp concert entertainment. I am glad that we worship the Triune God, for such a God who has ascended and descended and blows around like the wind will very likely be there with us in the middle of the night when the theology gets really tough.

* Sean McEvenue, *Interpretation*, 35, 1981, 236-7.

Lent 3
JOHN 4:5-42

Glory to You, Lord Christ

On more than one occasion, I have heard a bible reader conclude, "Here ends the reading" and the congregation respond, "Thanks be to God." For the next three weeks of Lent, we are privileged to read three long stories from John's Gospel. If they are read well in public worship, they will not need much of a sermon. Preachers will be getting worried that I am doing them out of a job, but I have heard people say that nothing works so well with a group of schoolchildren at Easter as reading straight through the Gospel story. I have kept an entire assembly quiet just by reading the raising of Lazarus from beginning to end.

So read on, and please, please, don't give in to the temptation to shorten these readings. Funny how we think it is more important to shorten the bible reading than the sermon. Which is really the word of the Lord?

Jesus at the well is very human and very worldly-wise. Tired out and thirsty, he sits and waits while his friends go off to find food in the town. He waits by the well until a local turns up. I have a lot to learn about ministry. When I am tired out I tend to go home, close the door, and phone for pizza home delivery. A friend who works in housing estates speaks of looking out for the "gatekeepers" in a community. You need to spend a lot of time with them, talking and listening. This woman may have been a gate-keeper. She not only was willing to shoot the breeze with the Galilean rabbi, but, perhaps even because of her five husbands, she was able to go back to her village and tell everyone else the gossip about him.

It is a story that rings true to life. On the other hand, it is a hard story to get a handle on. I find it hard to find a consistent thread in the conversation. You can't find three neat points to preach on. If God were trying to present revelation in the form of propositions and clear-cut doctrine, then he didn't do a very good job. It is the problem of story that it has ragged edges. But it is also the power of story.

The discussion left the Samaritan woman so intrigued that she went to get others to join in. What's more, it left Jesus so satisfied that he didn't want any food from his own friends. Here are hints that Jesus is already a true deacon working the fringes of society and enjoying it immensely. The in-group becomes rather sore at discovering it may no longer be the in-group.

Stories, like deacons, have ragged edges. They don't have a simple message. They can't be neatly labeled. In that they are rather like God and God's children. Which brings me to reiterate that warning I gave at the start: Don't dare give in to the temptation to shorten these stories for Lent as if to make the Gospel neater. Don't dare try to find the "essence" of this story and distill it in a shortened version. Leave the edges messy. Retell it, but don't box it in. Ask yourself, after the preacher has finished with it, whether this is still "the Gospel of the Lord."

Lent 4
JOHN 9:1-41
❧

The Eye of the Beholder

*T*his man is a real character. He may have been born blind, but like many streetwise people, he can see the situation clearly, with all its irony. He speaks simply, to the point: "I am the man," "He is a prophet." No wonder his parents would not speak for him. He has too much a mind of his own. At least, that's what this reader thinks about him and his story.

Recent theories of interpretation have focused on the reader of a text, rather than the writer or editor. We readers just can't help coming to the text and asking our questions of it. Some scholars suggest there may be as many "readings" of a text as there are readers, which sends us orthodox believers scrambling to nail down the truth (and nails come into this story somewhere else, don't they?). I believe that somewhere along the line, unless we enjoy being completely without an anchor for meaning, we need to also listen to the text, to be addressed by it. Of course truth itself ought not to be so easy to grasp hold of, considering we believe it is a person who constitutes the Truth.

This sighted man (he is not a blind man for most of the story despite the way we label him) meets a number of people who try to interpret him. The disciples suggest his meaning in life is as an example of God's curse. Jesus says he is an example of God's revelation. Neighbors suggest he is the blind beggar. Others say he is someone else. The sighted man says they are both right!

The Pharisees are more concerned to interpret the newcomer, Jesus, but they are blinkered from the start of their investigation and can only ever see the bias they bring. I feel even more sorry for the parents who boringly refuse to commit themselves to any interpretation, lest they make a mistake.

Meanwhile the sighted man continues to try out interpretations: a prophet? from God? or even, God? His parents were right to be frightened, because in the end he is driven out from the safety of blind orthodoxy. But his story has a happy ending. The One he was trying to interpret comes and seeks him out. With eyes fully opened, he worships the Truth. He has been interpreted by the One who sees most clearly of all, and his identity is neither blindman, beggar, sighted, neighbor, healed nor even witness. He is the child of God who has come home at last to his true parents.

And so we do our best to interpret the text, and sometimes we rejoice that our own biases and prejudices are the very means through which God speaks to us anew.

Thomas Cranmer had a theory known as Receptionism when it came to the Holy Communion. It makes a lot of sense to me when I am trying to locate the Truth in the bread and wine. It makes sense when I am trying to locate the Word of God in the text of scripture. What makes most sense of all to this blind person, is that the Truth, the Meaning, hears of my mess of meaning. The Truth seeks me out and asks his questions of me. That is what really matters in this whole business of understanding the text: that the text understands me.

Lent 5
JOHN 11:1-45
🌺

I Simply Won't Come Out

I don't think Martin Scorsese's film *The Last Temptation* deserved all the criticism it got, nor did it deserve all the hype. It went on for far too long and at the first sitting my strongest memory was of wishing it would end. Which says something about those who teetotal about such matters. I wouldn't have even seen it if they had not caused the furore.

Strangely though, I remember the film better than many others because of the images that have stuck with me over the years. I reckon that every preacher ought to watch movies if they want to communicate. People today think in images not words. One memorable image of Jesus was at the wedding in Cana. He sits chatting with friends while the miracle goes on behind him. At last he catches the eye of the master of ceremonies and gives him a kind of "I told you so" grin. Another scene has Jesus asking his disciples, as they try to convince him to deliver the sermon on the mount, "But what if I say the wrong thing?" and, even more terrified, "What if I say the right thing?"

The strongest and most lasting image, and it is strange because it wasn't quite as strong when I saw the movie a second time, was at the tomb of Lazarus. Jesus reaches his hand into the tomb and a hand reaches out of the darkness. There is a brief struggle of death with life. It is entirely possible that Lazarus could win, but Jesus finally drags him from the grave.

Later, Saul/Paul comes to murder Lazarus who is such an embarrassment to the Establishment. Lazarus is sitting outside his mudbrick dwelling, looking very pasty-faced, like death warmed up. Saul says, "Tell us, what was it like being dead?" Lazarus draws in another painful breath, "To tell you the truth, there was not much difference."

I still remember the day our Archbishop, David Penman, died in 1989. I heard a sermon on this passage of scripture. The preacher argued that the point for Martha was not whether there was life after death, but whether there was life before death. It was the most helpful thing I heard in that *annus horribilis*. It resulted in another poem:

LAZARUS' LULLABY
"At least I've got some peace now, some anonymity.
They've wrapped me tight in graveclothes, but funnily, I'm free.
I'm sorry for my sisters, that Jesus didn't come.
They thought he was Messiah, the Lord's anointed one.
I'm sorry for my wasted faith, that Jesus never came.
But what's it matter? Life and death, they're really much the same.
I'm sorry for the pain I felt, but that is in the past.
I'm dead. So what? It's no big deal. I've got some peace at last!
But what's that noise? The stone has moved and someone gives a shout.
Oh, shut the door! Pull down the blind! I simply won't come out!"

Passion / Palm Sunday
MATTHEW 26:14-27:66

Myths and Mistakes

I first read Matthew's account of the Passion, I mean really read it, when I had to read it without warning in front of a few hundred schoolchildren. I had honestly never noticed before the extraordinary additions by Matthew to the scene at the cross. I suppose we tend to merge and harmonize the stories of Christmas and Easter and assume they all say more or less the same thing. On that dreadful day I tried to read as quickly and unobtrusively as I could. Perhaps I could quietly slip past the tombs splitting open and the bodies of the saints being raised and walking about the city. On reflection I may have drawn more attention to it by trying to sound nonchalant.

These walking dead are an embarrassing little addition by our Gospel writer for the year. At least, it is embarrassing to us. It may have been perfectly understandable back then. To us it is another one of those signs that this was written for an audience 2000 years distant. For the sake of the integrity of that original audience, I don't want to pooh-pooh it too quickly. For the sake of that message, I don't want merely to explain it away as legend, myth or metaphor. Metaphors that hang around like this story has hung around for so many centuries have usually been hung on something tangible.

I have put off the moment for writing this Gospel Comment hoping that, if I waited long enough, another paragraph would leap out at me and demand comment. But I never seriously believed that would happen. These bodies walking around the city need to be dealt with. They have been around for a few years now and they demand my attention.

So masochistically I sit with these strange verses, and let them wash over me and around me. I watch Matthew's Passion with the many other women who looked on from a distance. Like them I am practically minded. I understand burial and funeral rites and common decency. But I will not hurry on to the tomb just yet.

I will sit at the cross with all its indecency, and I will sit at Matthew's cross with all the difficulties it causes my twentieth-century sceptical mind. It is dark, over the whole land, so I may not be seeing very well. Perhaps I simply imagined the dead walking around. Perhaps I invented the problem they cause me. There is an eerie silence. The man on the cross is muttering something about God or Elijah. He is screaming something totally incomprehensible. Finally he dies. The soldier says in his terror, "This was the Son of God."

How can such a one die without the world splitting open?

Easter
MATTHEW 28:1-10
❧

He is Not Here

*M*ark's ending is abrupt. The women arrive at the tomb, find it empty, and are afraid. Some of the faithful seem to have thought that version of the Good News needed more good news and did a swift steal from other stories around the resurrection. Personally I rather like Mark's abruptness, and the fear and doubt surrounding the tomb.

Luke's ending stretches into a lengthy walk to Emmaus, an appearance to the eleven, a whole second book, and in the end to the history of the church.

John can't quite decide when to end. He has many loose ends to tie up with Mary Magdalene, Galilee, and Simon Peter. In the end he doesn't do a bad job.

Matthew manages it in a mere 20 verses. In that sense it is an abrupt ending like Mark, but there is little time for doubt and fear at the tomb. Even with their doubt, the disciples are quickly sent out into the world by the first sighting of the risen Lord. There are few loose ends. The sorry tale of the guard at the tomb is explained away by officialdom. Matthew himself seems to have some sympathy for the plight of the soldiers with his angels and earthquakes causing them to become "like dead men." (There is a sermon somewhere around here about resurrections that cause people to become like the dead.)

The Easter story continues today. The disciples of Jesus go preaching and baptizing with worship and doubt in their hearts. Unbelievers continue to explain away events, even though it involves intricate and expensive schemes.

Meanwhile back at the tomb, the evidence for the good news, for the dissolution of fear and doubt, even though heralded by angels and earthquakes, is still that simple empty tomb. He is not here. Come, see the place where he lay.

Bend over and see the graveclothes as John bids you. Believe it or not. Don't be afraid of fear. Mark allows you to be a useless and speechless disciple. Disbelieve the idle tale all you like, says Luke, but beware of the risen Lord who may suddenly turn up at the dinner table. Understand the problems you are raising for the powers that be, warns Matthew. This mad story of resurrection is not just an embarrassment to individuals, but a threat to society.

If you are looking for Jesus this Easter, you may well be disappointed at first. We know you are looking for Jesus who was crucified. But he is not here. He has been raised. Come see the place where he lay.

Then follow this story to its proper end. Don't even stop to worry, like dead men, over angels and earthquakes. Just go quickly and tell.

Easter 2
JOHN 20:19-31

🌱

Low Sunday

I used to get quite cross around Easter when I taught school. All the pagan staff headed off for a break, but I found myself working hard over those same days and often coming back to work more weary than when I left. Easter worship is hard work. Worship is service.

I suppose one good reason for reading this passage every year on Low Sunday is that you could expect members of your congregation to chance upon it at least once in the cycle. I once heard a priest suggest he should take his annual leave at Eastertime because so few of his usual congregation were there in church. I do understand the need to head for the sea or the mountains. In Australia it is the last chance for reasonable weather before winter sets in. I am waiting for the day when the first Sunday after Easter becomes a real liturgical event in our calendar, when "Low Sunday" makes it officially.

On this first Easter night it is Jesus who causes all the trouble, as usual. It is a clear case of breaking and entering without the breaking. He turns up in that locked room and if they haven't already realized it, they will very soon learn which of the Jews they ought to be fearing most. Don't feel too sorry for this cosy club of disciples. The religious hierarchy isn't really after them. Not yet. They have more to fear from their risen Lord.

"Peace," he says. "Hallelujah," they reply, even after being shown the scars in his hands and side. "Peace," Jesus repeats, as if to say, "think twice before you rejoice so readily."

Then and there, he commissions them to go. In the process he gives them the best theological basis anyone could have for mission, namely the very nature of the sending God.

But they don't go. Next week they are still in the upper room, with doors shut. Not exactly open house. True, they have grown in number. Thomas has joined them. But that's not exactly evangelism explosion. Jesus shows the scars again. We next meet the disciples fishing up in Galilee. Not exactly what the Lord meant by sending, but at least they have opened the door of that room.

I wonder what would happen if everyone who stayed away from church on Low Sunday stayed away because they had decided to obey the great commission. What if they went off to their tents and holiday homes and forgave sins and brought shalom to their fellow holidaymakers. That would be a good basis for the celebration of the First Sunday after Easter.

It could give us an insight into all the other things that Jesus did that are not recorded in John's Gospel. Maybe all those caravan parks and seaside resorts are precisely the places where Jesus was making himself known in between visits to the upper room.

Easter 3
LUKE 24:13-35

Perfecting the Story

I have just asked someone who is preaching for his first time in our parish to preach on this Second Sunday after Easter. I said to him, "If you can't preach on the Road to Emmaus, you can't preach on anything." Now I think about it, it was a thoughtless piece of advice. These well-known passages are the hardest to preach on, precisely because they are so familiar.

All you have to do with this sermon is enable your audience to be there on the walk to Emmaus, to meet Jesus, to be encouraged on their walk, whether in despair walking away from Jerusalem, or in great joy having seen the risen Lord and running back to Jerusalem to tell the other disciples. Is that all?

Fortunately for us preachers, circumstances come together which have little to do with the hours of preparation put into a sermon. It happens to me occasionally when I come to the great high point of a sermon, about to move mountains or reduce people to tears. Someone will break into a fit of coughing, or a baby will cry uncontrollably, and the moment is lost. Last week, someone tipped over a vase of flowers for variation! I tried to ignore it, but it was a large vase and the water just kept glug-glugging out until we all dared to laugh at our seriousness. It puts you in your place and you realize the sermon, the story, is not merely "mine," or even "ours."

These folks from Emmaus have just heard Jesus opening the scriptures to them. They race back to the Eleven in Jerusalem and try to tell them their story. If we compare Mark's account of this story we discover, what seems to be behind Luke's version of the event, that the people at the top, the Eleven, didn't believe them. So much for sharing the story. So much for moving mountains.

On the other hand, the God of circumstances has also been known to arrange added extras to enliven the story. On one occasion when I preached on the Road to Emmaus, I was given a tape-recording of my efforts after the event. I was preaching away and there in the background I finally heard what my listeners had heard during the sermon, a bird singing through the chapel window. It was springtime, in the northern hemisphere where Easter's new life makes more sense. Even as I painted dark despair and blindness on the part of the two disciples, the bird began to chirp and it trilled away for the rest of the sermon. It was neither too loud nor too soft, just perfect background music. Only God could have arranged it so. Whether the Mr and Mrs Cleopas knew it or not, whether the Eleven knew it or not, whether I believed it or not, spring had sprung. Someone thanked me afterwards, not for my stunning sermon, but "for the whole event of worship." I could only smile.

The Eleven say, "The Lord is risen, he has appeared to Simon." The Cleopases say, "We've seen him too." In this telling of their separate stories, Jesus himself stood among them.

Easter 4
John 10:1-10

Mixed Messages

*T*here are some people you meet who manage to give you life, and some who seem to suck it out of you. It is not always obvious which is which. Jolly, vibrant people can sometimes leave you exhausted and lifeless, while very quiet and reflective people can send you off to climb Everest. I have observed that it has something to do with the ability to be in touch with pain. I remarked on this to a friend who smiled and showed me the necklace she wears with a crown of thorns and a dove. When I visit her, she tells me things about myself that I don't always want to know. I often cry in her company about my shortcomings and those of the world. But when I leave her, I feel empowered. She barely has to move a finger to do all this for me, and anyway she can't physically do much more than move a finger. She is in a wheelchair.

This section in my NRSV Bible is headed "Jesus the Good Shepherd," but it takes quite a while for Jesus to settle down to the analogy. He speaks of gatekeepers and gates and shepherds until we could become quite confused or think we have another piece of biblical evidence on which to base the doctrine of the Trinity. It is difficult to decide whose voice the sheep hear, the gatekeeper or the shepherd.

In first-century Palestine, in fact, the same person can easily be all three. We are talking here of an unsophisticated little stone-wall sheepfold, where the shepherd lies down across the doorway for the evening and becomes the gate. Who decides when to open and close the gate? Why, the gatekeeper of course, who is himself the gate.

Any thief would have to climb over the stones and disturb the sheep. Such a one comes only to steal and kill and destroy, though the thief may not know it is doing this. Presumably thieves are after sheep, or money, or possessions, or food on the table, with the purpose of making life more attractive and vibrant. It is just that in so doing they manage to suck the life out of others.

The gate is the way to nightly safety and to daily food. The gate achieves this by the simple act of opening at the right time and closing at the right time. Even more often the gate gives life just by being there. There is a lesson here for my Christian ministry, if only I could get the timing right.

This human gate becomes the shepherd who leads them to the pastures and home again at the end of the day. It is a living gate and a lifegiving gate, and sometimes it will need to give life at the expense of its own safety. Jesus could have mixed his metaphors even more, because this gate and shepherd is also the sheep who was slain, the Lamb of God.

I only have one problem with these mixed messages. What will happen to all the other sheep once the shepherd and gate is dead?

Easter 5
JOHN 14:1-14

🦂

Room with a View

I suppose everyone has a different view of heaven depending on their experience of earth. An Arab might naturally think of an oasis. A Somali could well imagine a safe haven with food and water, enough even for tomorrow. An Alaskan might think of a warm fireplace, which is interesting given our usual idea of hell.

Jesus speaks of dwelling places in the father's house. He has come from Galilee, lived at Capernaum, where today you can go and see the excavations of an insula. An insula was the kind of dwelling place pictured in the story of the friend at midnight, where a family had one room which they shared with their animals, Uncle Tom Cobbly and all. In an insula your one room was connected with many other families' rooms which combined to make one large community. Privacy was minimal. The Galilean disciples might well have imagined heaven as an uninterrupted sleep, or time and space to sit and think.

On the other hand, an insula must have afforded safety and communal spirit which would cause those same disciples to live uneasily behind our suburban walls and hedges. I can't imagine a desert dweller being happy in snow and ice for all eternity. I can imagine a refugee being totally terrified in one of our supermarket aisles.

Jesus speaks of dwelling places as he dines with his friends in Jerusalem. They are physically not too far from the over-large homes of the religious hierarchy up the hill, or the Roman governor's palace. Jesus would have seen Herod the Great's ridiculously expensive mountain dwelling as he gazed out past Bethlehem, and heard of the many other palaces of that megalomaniac in Jericho, Caesarea, and Masada.

Imagine, then, a safe communal dwelling with room to stretch out, with places for silence and reflection, but with family and friends never too far away. Imagine a place that does not need to be built on a mountain top to keep away the revolting masses, or with convenient window ledges to push your enemies over the edge. It may well have windows and height to catch the summer breezes, and beautifully tiled floors to cool your feet, but you won't have to be constantly looking over your shoulder or asking the food-taster to test the soup.

I have found myself caught lately in conversations about heaven. It is one of the things that non-Christians find puzzling and irrelevant about our faith. Nevertheless I have decided that heaven is vitally important to me not because my life here is so miserable, or because I am so other-worldly, but because there are things that I need to know will continue past the grave. Things like love and truth. It is not that I want a pie in the sky when I die. A meal of plain bread with loved ones will do just fine. A glass of wine would be a nice extra if it means that we can have a good discussion about things that really matter. Sound familiar?

Easter 6
JOHN 14:15-21

Me for You and You for Me

*I*n preparing this Comment, I gave in to the somewhat rationalistic urge to make a diagram of all the toing and froing of relationships mentioned in the reading. "You love me... you keep commandments... I will ask... the Father gives you... the Spirit will be with you... you know him... he abides with you... I will come to you... I live and you will live... you will know..." And so on. It very quickly got very messy as diagrams that have anything to do with the Holy Trinity are wont to do.

At last I began to see, almost despite the diagram, at least because of its messiness, that we who live in Jesus live in God. The toing and froing within God's nature, asking, giving, coming, loving, being, are mirrored in the life of the disciples of Christ as we are drawn into God's very being. If this is true, then obedience as the other side of love becomes much easier to comprehend.

Actually my diagram was not a great idea. Love is not a matter of drawing a line from one person to another which has a particular emotion attached. I know it is useful to remind ourselves that love is a matter of the will rather than the emotions, it is not just about feeling good. But neither is it detached, able to be turned on by a mere mental decision.

In this kind of attachment the lover is barely able to live without the beloved. "Because I live you also will live." Its reason for existence is tied up with the existence of the beloved. It feels orphaned when the beloved is absent. If this is the case with loving, then keeping the commandments of the beloved cannot be understood in a standoffish way either.

Such a connection between loving and obedience is much easier to comprehend. But it is also more devastating to discover its absence, because the connection between lover and beloved cannot be repaired by trying harder, either with heart or head. If the lack of obedience and love indicate that we are not living in God, there is not a lot to be done except despair. Orphans cannot do much about their sorry state.

My messy diagram came to the fore at precisely this point. The lines drawn from me to God were few. It is most wonderful to see my love for him so faint and poor. The lines from Father, Son and Spirit to me were many. It is most wonderful to know his love for me so free and sure. The God in whom we live will not leave us orphans.

Living in God is neither a matter of my emotions, nor even of my will, it is a matter of God's emotion and will. That love and obedience existed within the Godhead before I even was a twinkle in my father's eye.

Easter 7
(Ascension 1)
JOHN 17:1-11

✤

The Best of all Worlds

*T*he unity that Christ seeks for us is the same unity that Christ has with God. It has a lot to do with the glory Christ had in God's presence before the world began. This glory will be given by the Father to the Son, and will be handed on to his own people. All very cozy and shiny bright. It is cozy and bright until we realize that in John's version of good news, glory is seen preeminently in the cross, in the suffering of Jesus and thereby in the love that reaches out from God to the world.

The glory being spread around between God, Christ, and people, is a glory that has scars and pain attached.

I once asked God in a moment of particular agony whether this really was the best he could do in creating a world and why it hurt so much to love. In a time of deep grief I once read that "grief is love not wanting to let go." The phrase rang such bells that I obstinately refused to let go of my grieving lest I let go of my loving. I imagine I failed the psychologists at that point.

John's Gospel, with its glory in the cross, probably answers my questions as well as they can be answered this side of heaven. This universe is the best that God can do, because God's glory that existed before the world existed, means that in God's very nature is the cross. I know I am right out of my theological depth here and floundering desperately. The Moltmanns of the world have plumbed the depths of this kind of thinking far better than I ever can. All I can manage is to stutter and stammer about God and hurting being intimately connected. It hurts to love because that's what love is like, it hurts to love because that is what God is like.

Despite some interpretations of the 39 Articles of Religion, God is passionate. God may be without body, parts, and passions, but God is love, and love hurts, so God hurts, so glory is found in the cross. God, even before the world existed, was the kind of God that reached out in love and was liable to be hurt.

What a hard kind of prayer is this that prays for our unity to be like the unity of God, who is passionate, loving, and hurting? I detect a grieving in this prayer over what disciples are and will be. But if that is so, I trust that God also obstinately refuses to do the psychologically healthy thing and let go loving us.

One of the first weighty pastoral matters I had to deal with as a deacon was to help a teenager seeking an abortion. It was one of those dreadful lesser-of-two-evils situations. Everyone was relieved when it was over and nothing much was ever said again, but as I sat in the waiting room I read the available literature. Then I went home and wept.

"An abortion consists of removing the linings of the womb by suction and then checking the womb with an instrument not unlike a dessert spoon...The operation is over, usually in about ten minutes or so...How dangerous is an abortion? In the hands of specialists there is very little risk."

THE ABORTION

They just remove the linings. There is very little risk.
Each patient (if she pays) gets T.L.C.
You'll be back at work tomorrow. Your own doctor cannot tell.
Just sit back and enjoy your cup of tea.

It only takes ten minutes and they have three doctors here,
So, you see, they can do eighteen every hour.
It is safer now than childbirth and it beats the backyard job.
It is part of women's rights and women's power.

So why have I been crying when your problem is now gone?
My job was to support you, help you through.
It's not "aborting babies," it's "fertility control."
And after all, control is up to you.

The widow and the orphan, those who cannot help themselves,
Are the ones the Lord our God has pity on.
But I pity those who pity, for it's hell to mourn alone
Now the lining of your womb is dead and gone.

Pentecost
JOHN 20:19-23

O Comforter, Draw Near

*H*ang on, hang on, hang on. I don't want to spoil the flow of things, but I do have a few questions before we go much further. I don't think we should rush into this.

After all, Thomas is not here. Neither is Judas of course, but I guess you know about that. There's something lacking in the poetry with only the ten of us. Not that we aren't glad to see you again, but I just want to know what it is that you are about to breathe on us.

Resurrection? New life? That's fine. We could all use some new life right now. It's been a hard few years, not to mention the last week or so.

Peace? Yes, that's lovely. The world always needs peace. (Glad he's forgotten that bit about coming to bring a sword.) And sending? Yes, I think I see that. Just give us a couple of weeks to get over the trauma and shock, and we'll be out there convincing the world. Life and peace and sending come from God's own nature. We understand, we are to be God's own people in the world.

But let me ask my couple of questions. This is the same Spirit that you promised last week, isn't it. The Spirit of truth, the advocate, the helper, the one who will teach us everything and remind us of everything you said. That would be great. Sometimes you just packed in the information and I didn't have enough papyrus on me to take very full notes.

So, what's this business about sins, forgiving, retaining? Lord, surely you remember the trouble it caused when you went around claiming to forgive sins. They called it blasphemy. They wanted to have a nice little stoning at more than one spot in our schedule. I understand now that you are the Messiah the Son of the living God. You had every right to say those things. But we are mere mortals. How can we forgive sins?

And, forgive me for speaking so boldly, but I have had some experience, sin is not very popular at the moment. People don't like to be told they are sinners. Couldn't we just forgive them quietly and not tell them about it?

And last but not least, I was led to believe that God's forgiveness was open to all. This forgiving and retaining makes it look as if there are boundaries to be crossed between believers and unbelievers. I am sure I speak for the others when I say I would be very happy to preach forgiveness to all, but not to have this responsibility of retaining some sins.

If you want to breathe on us, then go right ahead. Just give us a double helping of peace and life and love and forgiveness for all. Hold the retaining of sins. It would be much simpler for all concerned.

Trinity Sunday
MATTHEW 28:16-20
(Some lectionaries use John 3:16-18,
see comment for Lent 2, pp. 49)

Have a Heart

Spirituality has been the "in" word for a while now. If you want to sell a religious book, just put "spirituality" somewhere in the title. Spirituality seems to be especially popular in affluent areas where people do not have to worry too much about the next meal, though the next restaurant might be causing a little concern. Such people probably have the luxury of seeing that life is more than money in the bank and a roof over the head. Life is more than physical and emotional well-being. There is an aspect of ourselves we can only call spiritual, and, if we are to be whole people, it needs nurturing.

This openness to spirituality gives quite an opportunity for our going and making disciples of all nations, and baptizing and teaching. It makes religion important in a world that used to be completely wrapped up in its worship of scientific technology. It makes the faith somehow comprehensible. If only we do not lose our nerve. Popular spirituality makes a good opening for our mission, so long as we realize that the opening is about the size of the human heart.

The final meeting with the risen Christ, according to Matthew, gives us spiritually aware people some room to maneuver. Even as we stand here and see Jesus with our own eyes, some of us worship, some doubt. Part of me worships, part doubts. And there is a flame, even in the doubting, that can be fanned into life. Call it spirituality, if you like. I can get a handle on that. It is about the size of the human heart.

The Christian faith and mission also has a huge element of incomprehensibility about it. This incomprehensibility is pretty much unavoidable because it is about the size of God. It is neatly summed up between Dorothy L. Sayers and the Athanasian Creed: "The Father incomprehensible, the Son incomprehensible, the Holy Ghost incomprehensible, and the whole lot incomprehensible." The size of the incomprehensibility of our faith makes Trinity Sunday the butt of preachers' jokes: "I never understand the Holy Trinity, so let me oversimplify with clover leaves or make it even more obscure with the names of German theologians. Suffer a little with me (I'll try to keep it short, but I need to speak long enough to show the length and breadth of my learning) and next week we will get back to the simple faith of Jesus."

Of course this simple faith of Jesus is rather too aggressive and definite to be politically correct. It is about direction, authority, teaching, obedience, and commandments. Not a lot of consultation involved. The simple faith of Jesus is what makes our faith incomprehensible. We old disciples baptize new disciples by drowning them in water. We obedient followers constantly celebrate the death of the one who followed God with complete obedience.

We do have a space in our hearts for God, a space that needs filling. It makes the human need for religion understandable. But on this incomprehensible Sunday, more important is the space that exists for us in the heart of the Triune God.

The Body and Blood of Christ
JOHN 6:51-58

Bringing a Sword

The years of discussing the possibility of priesting women in our church were not easy. It seemed that history was repeating itself in the way such huge outbursts of anger arose over the body and blood of Christ. Nor have the first few years of having women priests in our church been easy. Some people thought that we would have really arrived the day women were priested. Some local parish churches thought they really wanted a woman priest. But none of us knew what we were talking about, because it remains to be seen, it is only being worked out gradually what a woman priest actually is!

I remember reading the results of a survey taken in New Zealand after some years of women priests. A huge percentage of people couldn't remember what the arguments were all about. One respondent who still did not agree with the idea gave as his reason, "Women make God too human, too accessible." I have found myself criticized for the same thing. I tried for a time to back down and become a bit more deep and meaningful, but it was not authentic me. Like it or not, my style is pretty friendly. I reckon God has enough mystery about him without my additions.

It seems that between churches, within churches, we are destined always to be fighting over the Lord's Supper, over the body of Christ, over who owns the church. It is akin to the disputes that arose for Jesus after the great miracle of feeding and Jesus' words to the crowds who sought him out and asked him what he was doing. As a result of his words, the Jewish leaders complained about Jesus, because he said, "I am the bread that came down from heaven." Unlike me, Jesus did not back down. If those who held the power in the church were bothered before, Jesus makes it crystal clear that the extraordinary claims are indeed as extraordinary as they had at first sounded.

In reaction to his reply the leaders begin to dispute among themselves. Jesus brings a sword and I can't help wondering how difficult he found it hearing their internal disputes. Jesus continues to break in on their discussion by making even more crass and physical claims about his body and his blood. It is as if he is saying, "Look, if you want to fight about this, make sure you fight about the things that really matter."

His disciples find the words difficult and begin to drift away. Only those who simply have to stay will remain, and they can give no solid reason. Some of their motives will turn out to be on very shaky ground indeed. The powerful people begin to scheme concerning the body and blood of Christ, to rid themselves of the problem.

It distresses me that people still argue vehemently in our chuches, but often it is because the body and blood of Christ really matter. It matters that a celebration of the Body and Blood of Christ stirs in us the realization that we disciples do not all share in the one bread, and that not all have heard of the benefits of the death of the one who caused the first arguments over body and blood.

Proper 4
(Ordinary Sunday 9)
MATTHEW 7:21-29

❧

Not Only with Our Lips

*W*e have arrived at the end of the Sermon on the Mount. Jesus has finished his long period of teaching and, unlike the readers of Mark, we are now in a position to decide for ourselves whether we share the astonishment of the crowds. This is a vital question for us, for we are warned about the end of those who build the structure of their lives on flimsy foundations.

But what is the rock? What is the foundation? Paul tells us elsewhere that Christ is the rock and that cannot be far from the truth here. But perhaps even more for Matthew the foundation is expressed in the repeated phrase "these words of mine." The teaching of Jesus, this sermon on the mountain, are the solid foundation we need, lest we become like those who cry "Lord, Lord," and yet remain unrecognizable to Jesus, and fail to enter the kingdom.

However, this foundation of teaching needs a little more explanation. There have been many who have based their lives on teaching, even the teaching of Jesus, who have sadly missed the point. Matthew rails against false prophets who lead many astray (24:12) and whose lawlessness finally denies the great commandment of the law which is to love. They may even claim to prophesy in the name of Jesus. To all appearances they are part of the community of faith.

This teaching of Jesus is not just about knowing the right words, but doing the right actions. The sermon is followed immediately by a healing of an outsider who is told not to speak but to obey the law, by the healing of a servant whose master understands the close connection between word and deed, and the healing of a woman whose first action is to serve Jesus.

The connection between word and action cannot be the kind of legalism that ties heavy burdens upon others, that acts only for the benefit that accrues for the actor (23:4-5). Nevertheless even while condemning that attitude of the Scribes and Pharisees, Jesus tells the crowds to do whatever teaching they receive from the seat of Moses and follow it.

Christians have tried many ways to hold together teaching and action, commandments and obedience, words and life, but there is a very fine line between lawlessness and legalism. How is it possible to follow this teaching of Jesus without despairing, for it makes all the law and the prophets sound like child's play? The eschatological dimension with which Jesus ends his sermon gives us the clue. Just as I now see in a mirror dimly, so I act now in a mirror dimly. My obedience is partly realized, but it awaits its fulfillment on the last day when I will know as I am known and rejoice to do as I am commanded.

Proper 5
(Ordinary Sunday 10)
MATTHEW 9:9-13, 18-26

✤

Got a Minute?

Other clergy are the worst offenders who phone you at mealtimes. I suppose they know when to catch you at home. If you leave the answering machine on, some people will even say, "Come on, pick up the phone, I know you're there!" Some days I cope better with the interruptions, some days I get rather irritable.

I was talking to a woman who had just begun a new job with some elderly residents in a local hostel. She was officially called "Activities Co-ordinator" and was supposed to get everyone involved in painting, basket weaving, pottery, bingo, aerobics, singalongs, you name it. She told me that, after a whole month in the job, she had not yet managed to organize any activity because she had spent all her time just talking with the people in her care. I consoled her by suggesting that was what they wanted and needed. Someone listening in on the conversation said wisely to her, "Your ministry is what you do between the times you are doing your job." So she continued her ministry happily until the job finally fitted in. The residents were happy and well-cared-for, and appreciated her job and her ministry.

I remind myself of those wise words every time I get annoyed by interruptions. Oh, I know you have to plan your weeks and days so that you do eventually achieve your goals. But we read here that interruptions are part of what Jesus brings and allowance should be made for them in the great timetable of life.

Jesus was the first to interrupt. He saw Matthew at his job and gave him a ministry instead. The miracle is that Matthew simply got up and followed this one who brought new life. Jesus was interrupted at his dinner with the extraordinary request to go and heal a young girl who had died. That journey was interrupted by another person in desperate need. Finally the ministry of the mourners was interrupted by life itself coming into their midst.

But Matthew tells this series of stories so simply and quietly that we could well miss the point. Matthew got up without a word and followed. Jesus got up without a word and followed. He told the frenzied crowd, "Go away." New life comes immediately, silently, without commotion. The woman was healed by a touch. Jesus simply commended her for her faith. The girl was not dead, only sleeping, and once the musicians and wailers were dismissed, she got up.

The story was told noisily throughout the district, but the events themselves were quiet. The interruptions spring up before you and demand attention, or they follow you around silently clutching at your coattails. Our real ministry is mostly quiet because faith that simply gets up and follows the call is mostly quiet. Even miraculous new life comes without commotion.

Proper 6
(Ordinary Sunday 11)
MATTHEW 9:35-10:8

※

Back to the Future

*T*he latest thing in hermeneutics, or at least the latest thing I have read, says that the meaning of a text is not in the world behind the text, nor in the author of the text, nor even in the text itself, but in the world in front of the text, the world which the text calls into being. Meaning, and revelation, is not back there. If it is just back there, then it is probably quite irrelevant to my concerns. If meaning is right here, even that will not help because, as soon I say it, the moment has passed. It's like asking a person what is the correct time. It is impossible to answer. But if meaning is out ahead, in the future, then there are possibilities not only for our understanding, but for our action. Strange that a text from such an ancient time can continue to work out a future for its readers. That's why it is regarded as a classic.

The $64,000 question is what world this particular text from Matthew is calling into being, where it is calling us, what is out there.

Into compassion. Jesus had compassion on the leaderless crowds and it seems reasonable to expect that his friends also will have compassion. And I do. It's just that I had thought he would spend more time with his close friends first.

Into prayer. You have probably noticed already how dangerous it is to pray. If God takes your request at all seriously you are likely to find yourself at the center of an answer to your own prayer. Jesus asked his friends to pray for the sheep. The result was the commissioning of twelve of them to do something about the flock. The Twelve, beginning with the rock and ending with the betrayer. And, yes, says the tax collector, I was there too, about halfway between.

Into learning. Before they go out they will get a chapter's worth of teaching from the Great Shepherd. This might be important, folks, so pay close attention to Matthew chapter 10. There's rather a lot about judgment, wolves, betrayal, slaves, fear, and swords. Sorry. No money in it, either.

Into action. Proclaiming, curing, raising, cleansing, casting out, giving. Strange and specially directed action that we now regard as snobbish if not racist. At least it sets limits so we don't think we are meant to do everything all at once.

Into crisis. After the teaching they will go off into what Frank Moloney calls the coming crisis of the Messiah's ministry.* That will involve a whole new way of thinking and speaking. It will be so critical a time that even Jesus will find the need to withdraw occasionally.

Rather a lot of calling. Rather a big world for one little text to create. Just as well it is only directed to the twelve apostles back there.

* Francis J. Moloney, *This is the Gospel of the Lord Year A*, St Pauls Publications, Homebush, NSW, 1992, 35.

Proper 7
(Ordinary Sunday 12)
MATTHEW 10:24-39

Now I Lay Me Down to Sleep

When I was little, my brother and I would whisper into the night as children often do. I would sometimes get fits of giggling that drove my mother mad, especially if I were giggling well past my bedtime. My brother obviously had more self-control than I did, but I sometimes giggled so much that it was very hard to stop. When I heard Mum coming up the hall, I would think of the most awful thing I could in order to avoid trouble. It always worked, but the cure was worse than the disease. I would think of the devil coming to get me. When Mum put her head around the bedroom door, it was not for fear of her that I cowered under the bedclothes, quiet as a mouse. I didn't use that cure too often because I found I couldn't get up a good giggle again for weeks afterwards.

Now I am older, I have put away childish things. I am scared of grown-up things: like going gray, though I already am; like losing my mind, but maybe I already am, and anyway how would I know if I were; not being liked, but we can't please everyone all the time, and no one loves a lowest common denominator; losing my loved ones, but even those who put up with my odd ways and love me in spite of or because of them, even they won't always be here. Maybe the child in me was more perceptive after all.

Whom to fear, says my grammatically precise NRSV. It matters most for disciples that they are on the side of Jesus. Any moment now, whispers will turn into shouts, rumors will turn into reality, and if you think the master has been getting in trouble for his preaching, you ain't seen nothin' yet. Nevertheless there is only one person to worry about pleasing. There is only one person to bring you back down to earth or raise you up to heaven, and it is not the devil coming to get you.

I hope you get something out of these Gospel Comments. They work on me occasionally. The other night I woke up with a sense of something enormously terrifying in the room, far too big for a burglar. I remember back in Lent I wrote about another scary experience "How did you know it wasn't God?" I sensed a huge cloud move over me and I had a sense that something in the universe had moved significantly. I couldn't think of much to tell my poor husband who had been rudely wakened, except to give him the stunning piece of advice that on Sunday when he was due to preach he should just "Tell them about Jesus." Despite my tears I had a sense of great well-being and fell quickly back into a deep sleep. I just had time to feel vaguely surprised that I found no need to cover my head with the blankets.

Whom to follow? What to preach? Whom to fear? Life is pretty simple really, and the answers to the really deep questions remain the same. Even if the hairs on my head are going gray, they are still counted. Even if my mind is going, I know I am loved. I know because my mother has just walked up the hall to see that I am sleeping soundly.

Proper 8
(Ordinary Sunday 13)
MATTHEW 10: 40-42

Blood and Water

*I*think it was Ogden Nash who wrote "Blood is thicker than water, and so it oughta." He was referring to the fact that we can choose our friends, but we are stuck with our relatives. On the other hand, friendships come and go, they blossom and die, and year after year we eat Christmas dinner with our families even if we would rather spend it with our friends. In most families you still turn up for a funeral even if you didn't see much of "the old fellow" during his lifetime.

We didn't need Dr Freud to tell us that, when families don't work well, they cause problems unto the third and fourth generation. When families work well, they give great support in times of need and provide an appropriate setting for celebrations. There is something realistic about being stuck with a group of people.

When Jesus talks about family and bloodlines, everything is different. Swords and crucifixions abound, and they relate to blood in quite a different way. This Messiah is coming to overturn more than money tables in the temple. Losing life will be the way to find life. It's not that Jesus has anything against families as such. It's just that we ought to understand that this hound of heaven doesn't want our blood ties, he wants our lifeblood.

Our new blood-brother relationship with Jesus is so close that we disciples can be mistaken for Jesus himself. The one who welcomes a prophet is like a prophet, the one who welcomes a righteous person is righteous. And, lest you think merely in terms of rewards for welcoming the right sort of person home to dinner, the one who gives a drink of cold water to a little one will be rewarded. I have no idea what the reward of a little one will be, but I seem to remember somewhere Jesus made a big point about little ones and entering the kingdom.

We are stuck with our family and it is therefore appropriate to speak of the church as family. God works in such mysterious ways from a human point of view that he doesn't appear to have any taste at all when it comes to choosing friends. We find ourselves in a pew on Sunday sitting next to all sorts and conditions of men and women. Not the usual sort you would invite home to lunch.

I am not sure what the old saying means that water is thinner than blood. Could it be baptism? If so, the saying is quite wrong. The Gospel sacraments involve both water and blood. We join our new family in a watery way. We continue to live in it by body and blood.

In this coming kingdom of heaven, blood may no longer be thicker than water. It all depends on the sort of blood and water we are talking about.

Proper 9
(Ordinary Sunday 14)
MATTHEW 11:16-19, 25-30

Meaning?

*T*o sound knowledgeable in hermeneutics you need to know about "the intentional fallacy." It is a fancy way of saying that it is a mistake to try to discover the intention of the author of a text as something which lurks mysteriously behind the text. The author's intention, or as much as we can know of it, is right before our eyes in the text.

Now, I personally don't mind friends helping me out occasionally when I stumble over words and meaning. I appreciate them saying, "What she really means is..." It's rather like a translation for those who don't speak my odd lingo. Since I often open my mouth just to change feet, I am glad for the escape clause. But it can also become patronizing and then I have to object, "No, I really meant just what I said."

Commentators on bible verses need to do a lot of the former: translating for us, because of differences in language and culture. Commentators on bible verses also need to know when to stop lest they smugly patronize those who originally wrote the scriptures and those who now read them simply to discover God's will.

This particular text makes its intentions pretty clear. The wise and intelligent don't get the message. Infants do. It is not that the wise and clever people are put in second place with this message. They don't seem to get a place at all! Babies are where it is at, and for this Jesus thanks the Lord of heaven and earth. It is exactly what God meant to happen. It is exactly what grace intended.

It is easy to talk in terms of metaphor and parable: Jesus really meant that the simpler folk receive revelation, fishermen rather than rabbis. Jesus is using hyperbole to show that we must not think too highly of ourselves. But the fact remains that Jesus actually says "hidden from the wise" and "revealed to babies" and that this is God's will. I fear being so wise about his words that I miss his revelation. The one thing that any theory of interpretation has to explain is that great scholars sometimes manage to miss the meaning of the bible while the common folk manage to see it as clear as the day.

Jesus is content to think of himself as a son to his father. If it's good enough for Jesus, I ought to be content to think of myself as a baby. Unless I really want to continue with this self-imposed heavy load.

"What he really means" can be a loud and pompous way of refusing to listen to the still, small voice of God. Sometimes the clear, plain meaning is just too simple for words. Jesus is just too gentle and humble to follow and his demands are too easy and light to be worth the bother.

Lord, let me never be too old and intelligent for your grace.

Proper 10
(Ordinary Sunday 15)
MATTHEW 13:1-23

Dangerous Talk

*H*ow do you get through to people who are in desperate need of help, but unable to hear when help is offered? A whole new way of speaking is called for. Parables.

As a school chaplain I used to speak at school assemblies every week and soon saw the soul-destroying way children would turn off at "the religious bit." They liked to hear about people, even about me, but as soon as you moved from "real life" to the bible message, the shutters came down with a crunch.

So I tried telling parables. At least, I thought they were parables. On one occasion I told about my garden, how it had plants that liked to be fussed over and plants that liked to be left alone. Some thrived in damp muddy places, others liked it hot and dry. I pointed out that Mary Magdalene thought Jesus was the gardener and I thought she was correct. The unspoken point was that Jesus cared for them all no matter how different they were. It was an assembly talk that had them nicely confused as to which was the religious bit.

They didn't turn off. They were mostly puzzled. A few weeks later a Year Ten girl, for whom, you must understand, it is anathema to listen in assembly, sought me out to talk about one of my trees, a rather sick maple. She had gone home and told her parents about assembly and had come back with some horticultural advice. I smiled sweetly because she had missed the point.

It took a few more such stories and incidents before I realized I was the one missing the point. I had not been telling parables but allegories, stories in which I kept control of the meaning. Jesus, who has always been smarter than I, was willing to let go of the meaning. Here's a story which relates to your world; come into the story with me, and let's see what happens. But remember, you are taking a risk, your world might be turned on its head. If you want to know what I had in mind when I told the story, then I will tell you, but I am just as willing to hear your ideas.

In the long run the parable opens up a conversation. If it is a true conversation we cannot tell ahead of time where it will go. I am slowly learning to allow for God's Spirit. The garden metaphors had a lot of mileage for the early Christians. I too have found them extraordinarily creative. I am slowly learning to handle the responses. When I told the people of my parish about my gardening attempts, one person, a poet who should have known better, offered to take over the gardening around the church. I happily accepted! The church garden now looks terrific.

But, God forgive me, I should have conversed with that Year Ten girl and cultivated her interest in gardening. I can only hope she continues to take an interest and has met the more expert gardener.

Proper 11
(Ordinary Sunday 16)
MATTHEW 13:24-43

Weeds and Seeds

*T*his gardening is a delicate business. I worry a lot over my plants. I worry over the weeds too. How do you tell a weed from a plant apart from the fact that the snails eat the plants and leave the weeds? They say a weed is only a plant growing in the wrong place, which means they can also be identified by their speedier than usual growth rate. But have you ever seen orange nasturiums growing out of control alongside the railway track, or white Queen Anne's lace by the road or a bed of blue forget-me-nots that have taken over? It's the lilies of the field all over again.

My mother always told me not to dig over a garden in a new house too quickly until you see what comes up in the way of bulbs. It's good advice if you can stop yourself from making it all too neat too quickly. It's better to potter around at ground level for a while. If only you can tell the weeds from the plants. A lot can be achieved by mulching.

I am currently working on azaleas. I have only ever killed them off before now. I consulted a friend who grows fabulous bushes and he told me they like leaf mould. We have leaf mould in abundance in our present home so I planted them and piled up the leaves. I do believe my azaleas have grown a few inches since last year. Mostly because I left them alone.

The weeds seem to leave them alone too.

My best experience with azaleas was in a house we only lived in for a few months. I was in a pretty fragile condition, but those old established azaleas just bloomed and bloomed. People asked us what we did to make them so lovely. We just sipped tea on the porch and enjoyed them. Seasons since then people tell us they have never been quite so good.

That was one good garden. It seemed to know I needed the sustenance. My neighbor saw I liked the garden so she gave me some leftover tomato plants over the fence. I put them along the side of the house, partly because I was too embarrassed to put them in a sensible spot in the open lest they wither away. They grew more tomatoes than the neighbor's plants and she was not a little green over the fence. People asked us what we did to make our tomatoes so saucy. We just smiled and offered them another bagful to take home. I think they were still producing when we packed the moving van.

I am getting to the stage, some call it old age, when I reckon gardening is more about reading the signs than digging in the compost. Each year I find myself saying, "It is a good year for jasmine, or acacia, or roses, or whatever is doing well." When you see everyone's azaleas looking great it must have more to do with the season than the individual gardeners. I have had one year success stories with sweet peas and dahlias that have been unrepeatable forever after. It was not mere luck. It was simply a good year for sweet peas.

I just hope this is going to be a good year for azaleas.

Proper 12
(Ordinary Sunday 17)
MATTHEW 13:31-33, 44-52

꽃

Finders Keepers?

I found this story of treasure in the field some eight years ago, and it meant a lot to me. But meaning is quicksilver. It cannot be held selfishly. I can't help wondering what it means now for scribes and householders who bring out new and old:

There was once a woman who was digging in the field. As she worked amongst the dirt and weeds, she uncovered an unusual stone. She turned it over carefully, wiped it with her handkerchief and examined it. She took it to the faucet and gently rinsed it off. It shone strangely in the sunshine, and suddenly her heart was filled with joy. She felt sure it was a diamond. She ran to her neighbors and said, rather biblically, "Rejoice with me for I have found a diamond in the field."

Some workmates looked at it and said, "Oh yes, it's beautiful. But what are you going to do with it? You don't wear diamonds, do you?" Others said, "No it can't be a diamond. No one ever found a diamond in that field before and people have been digging there for centuries." "Just look at it," they said, as they passed it around. "How do you know if it's a diamond?" someone asked. She waited patiently while they examined it.

"You're confused with the news from the next town," someone

suggested. "I heard they found diamonds there." "Yes," said another, "and look where it got them. They haven't stopped fighting about diamonds ever since."

When she finally got her stone back, it was looking rather grubby and sweaty, so she quickly put it in her pocket and went back to her digging in the field.

As the days passed she almost forgot about her stone. Occasionally other people would mention diamonds and she would put her hand quietly in her pocket and think to herself, "It must be a diamond." She began to think less and less about it. Even if a friend said, "Whatever happened to that stone you found?" she would just shrug and say, "Oh, that."

But one day a stranger came to town, a woman dressed in unusual clothing with a bright gleam in her eyes. "The time for diamonds is here," she cried out. "I have a diamond and it has been cut and polished. Look how it shines. Get out your stones and bring them to be cut and polished too."

The woman listened in amazement. She fingered the stone in her pocket. As she looked around, she began to realize that many others also stood and listened to the newcomer. They too seemed to be ready to reach into their pockets.

"If only I could be sure," the woman thought. "If I get out my stone to be polished, will they produce theirs too?"

And she hesitated.

Proper 13
(Ordinary Sunday 18)
MATTHEW 14:13-21

❧

Out of Control

*T*hank goodness all those stories are finished. I am trying to preach biblically, but preaching on parables is next to impossible. When I say "preach biblically" I do not mean merely to sprinkle bible passages through every paragraph. I mean to ask what the text does or affects, and then aim my sermon to do the same kinds of things. Those parables were getting out of control. They might have been fun, but there seemed to be no telling what they meant or where they were leading. I would have thought God meant us to have more control over our preaching, over our words, than that.

Here we are at last back to the real story, Jesus moving around again, getting on with his mission, teaching his disciples, healing and helping and preaching the good news. It ought to be easier now simply to preach about what happened. However, even this history, this biography, is told as a story, with the aim of doing something to us. And this particular part of the story gives us hints that control is not so easy as we might imagine.

The Word himself withdraws and tries to take a pause from the story to regroup after hearing of the cruel death of a friend. The Word is silent, the Preacher cannot continue. Perhaps he glimpses, in the meaningless death of the Baptist, the forces that will soon rob him of all control. If there is a message about biblical preaching here, it is that effective preaching can lead to the death of the preacher. It comes as no surprise, then, that the Word loses control of this moment as the crowds follow him, intruding into his private space, demanding more and more.

The disciples cannot be faulted for their care of the crowds and of their master. Sending the crowds away will help both their hunger for food and his hunger for peace. "You give them something to eat," the Word speaks at last, and they must reveal their lack of resources. "You give them something to eat," the Word once said to me, when I wanted to run and hide after the tragic death of a young relative. So we, the disciples and I, brought out our "nothing much," and revealed our emptiness. But we brought it to Jesus who gave thanks and fed the crowds.

I imagine the twelve disciples grumbling a little as they clean up the leftovers, "You'd think someone who could do such a miracle could get the amounts right." If they did so grumble they missed the point that he did get the amounts right, exactly right. Of course miracles are difficult to keep under control. Any minute now he'll be striding out across the lake.

The Protestant in me likes words. The English graduate in me likes words. The storyteller in me likes words. Words do things. But today's story may well be more out of control than any parable. Here God's Word does things out of his silence and grief, out of his compassion, out of his companions' bewildering lack of possibilities. Out of control.

Proper 14
(Ordinary Sunday 19)
MATTHEW 14: 22-33

❧

Not a Minute Less

*I*n the olden days, when we went to the beach with our parents, there was one golden rule. Whatever else you did, you must never, never go into the water until a full hour had passed since lunch. Not even up to your ankles. Fifty-nine minutes was not good enough. It had to be the full sixty minutes. I never actually saw what happened to wicked children who did break the sixty-minute rule, but I was led to imagine some dreadful agony happening even in shallow water because lunch "hadn't gone down yet." I blame my parents and those beach outings for my adult fetish for punctuality.

How times have changed. Now they tell me it may cause cramps to go swimming on an empty stomach. Whatever my pseudo-medical knowledge may be, Matthew tells us that the water incident with Jesus happened "immediately" after the eating one. I imagine the connection between the two is much more profound than my mother's stopwatch.

That whole incident with the loaves and fish reminded me of the picnic that Moses and the elders had with God on the side of the mountain. You'll remember they saw the pavement under God's feet like sapphire. I wish I could see some sapphire pavement under my feet right now. All we can see is black watery chaos under our boat.

Late this afternoon Jesus ordered us disciples into this boat, out onto the lake. He said he would handle the crowds. Thank goodness. Personally I am rather tired of their demands. It seemed a good idea to set sail at the time, but perhaps his timing was out after all. A wind has blown down out of the Golan Heights, as it often does without warning, and our boat is taking on water. We have gotten rid of all the excess baggage we could. This has happened before, you know.

I don't like to complain but I suspect one of the others has brought those twelve baskets of leftovers with him. Probably hopes to outsell the hot bread shop in the morning. Twelve baskets can be heavy and awkward, and I rather wish he hadn't stowed them away. For that matter some of the more burly fellows ate rather a lot for dinner. And some of them are losing it all now in the rough sea.

I know you are thinking I should have more faith. We've been in this situation before. But it's not quite like last time the going got rough on this lake. Jesus was physically with us then. Asleep in the back of the boat, but with us, and able to do something at the crucial moment. Tonight he said something about going up a mountain to pray. Moses went up the mountain for forty days after his picnic with the elders. He did eventually come back with the ten commandments. I would happily obey a command or two from the great I AM right now if it would get us out of this storm.

Proper 15
(Ordinary Sunday 20)
MATTHEW 15:21-28

Answering Back

*T*he step-by-step creation of human beings in Genesis chapter two provides an interesting list of characteristics that completes humanity by the end of the chapter. They will have a close relationship with the earth, they will have the breath of God, work, companionship, speech, sleep, each other, and song. This must be at least part of what it means to be created in the image of God.

Speech is Godlike. The epistle of James warns of the danger of the unbridled tongue, nevertheless it is surely a case of a great evil coming from the corruption of a great good.

The psalms of Israel encourage me to speak up, and to sing. To speak my most painful nightmares and to sing the blues. To speak my wildest dreams and to rejoice. Psalm 39 is particularly encouraging to those who think God only wants to hear our refined and joyful praise. Perhaps the most encouraging thing about human speech is that God's own holy word dares to consist of our faltering words.

The creation story reminds us that God's word is powerful: let there be light and there was light. In the garden the humans enjoy an evening stroll and chat with their creator: communion. However, Walter

Brueggemann reminds us of another way of looking at this speaking that goes on between people and God. "It is commonly assumed that it is the speech of God that makes communion possible. That is, communion results from divine initiative. That is sometimes true. As we shall see, however, the speech of Israel can also initiate communion, when it is speech that is as bold as it is faithful." *

Preachers, like the psalmist and like God, are not those who speak simply because they like the sound of their own voice. They are rather those who give voice to those unable to speak for themselves, who encourage quiet ones to speak up, who enable those in great need to scream out their pain.

The closest disciples are often embarrassed by such outbursts from the fringe dwellers. We assume that God prefers our psalms of praise. But God's word, the word written and the Word walking about on earth, engages with this pain, teasing it out, throwing orthodox theology in its face, arguing with it, standing up to it, treating it as fully human by confronting it just as it has dared to confront God.

If my hypothesis about human speech is even halfway true, then this noisy Canaanite woman must have pleased God's Word immensely. She has just the right attitude. She shouts until he answers, then she kneels before him and continues to engage in give and take, even from her humble position. Her language may not have been politically correct as far as the "gender police" are concerned. But her daughter was healed instantly because she had great faith, because she had the gall to argue with God.

WHAT LANGUAGE SHALL I USE?

Mother, Father, Parent God, Lord of all we do or say,
Word Incarnate, Holy Spirit, teach your children how to pray.
Cherubim and seraphim, angels praise your holy name.
We are time- and space-bound creatures. Shall we dare to do the
   same?
Words and creeds cannot contain you, let alone a finite mind.
You who cast out evil spirits, healed the deaf, the dumb, the blind,

You who made the lame go walking, loose our tongues and set us free.
Let us bravely speak about you, be it by analogy.

Jesus dared to walk among us, trapped in all our words and ways,
Help us follow that example. Help us find the words for praise.
Help us find the words that build up. Help us share each other's pain.
Mother, Father, Parent God, teach us how to pray again.

* Walter Brueggemann *Finally Comes the Poet: Daring Speech for Proclamation*, Fortress Press, Minneapolis, 1989, 50.

Proper 16
(Ordinary Sunday 21)
MATTHEW 16:13-20

🌿

Making Connections

*T*he disciples have finally understood the significance of the yeast and the bread. Perhaps they will also now understand the significance of the loaves and the fish and the baskets of leftovers. They are ready to make other vital connections. They will make the great confession of Caesarea Philippi, and on this rock the church will be built.

It is therefore with some reluctance that I admit my ignorance of the complete significance of the miracles and the conversation in the boat. Certainly, I understand that there is more than yeasty bread involved here, but I am not at all sure about the seven and twelve baskets or the numbers of loaves and the fish. Being ignorant I, like Peter, am probably about to misunderstand my own realization that I am conversing with the Christ, the Messiah, the Son of the living God. I am likely to misunderstand the necessity of where we are headed in this strange journey.

Perhaps it would be better if I were not so forthright in my answers to his questions. I will answer for others freely enough, but I am reluctant to speak my own thoughts openly and honestly lest I make a fool of myself, and worse, lest I make a fool of my friend and teacher.

Common sense tells me that this man cannot be anything but a man.

We have traveled with him, we have seen him tired at the end of a long day. We have even done our best to protect him from the masses who merely want to use him for their own ends and suck the lifeblood out of him. He is human, like us. Son of Man. (Or is it Son of God? I can never remember which title refers more to his humanity and which is the divine title.) And yet common sense also tells me that he is more than a man. He takes our inadequacies, our meager resources, and feeds thousands. He is different. He is the Christ. Our people have been waiting for this one for hundreds of years. We know what we mean by the concept of the Christ, and Matthew's telling of the incident lets us know that there is more to Jesus than a political entity. Son of Man is also Son of the living God.

And yet, at the end of the conversation, Jesus tells us to be silent. Our silence is not necessarily because we will say something stupid and ruin the whole mission. (We will probably do that anyway!) The silence is because of the connection between humanity and heaven. There is a sense in which we have worked it out for ourselves. Son of Man, Son of God; a man, yet different from any other man; God who walks around within creation. But knowing God is only possible if God reveals himself. We are now no longer in the realm of logic. We are talking, we are doing, theo-logic. We are in the heavenly realms.

This talking and doing true theology has within it a large amount of silence as well as speech.

Proper 17
(Ordinary Sunday 22)
MATTHEW 16:21-28

❧

Cross Purposes

*I*t has been revealed to us that this Jesus is the Christ, the Son of the Living God. We are pretty pleased with ourselves, though we have no real reason to be proud, because revelation is revelation and not self-discovery. However, we do think Jesus was pretty pleased with us too. He told us that our confession is like a foundation, a huge substrata, a rock on which to build. Who knows what will be built in the next few years. He has treated our newfound understanding like a turning point in our travels. I can feel it in my bones. We are really going to make it happen now.

But that only makes me wonder more. What is to happen up ahead? With those charges of blasphemy that the religious legalists are always trying to pin on him, it is quite possible that a stoning will occur. We have had a few near escapes already. I don't fancy a stoning. You don't often see them these days. People are much more liberal in their attitudes, not so desperate to force religion down your neck, at least not in the form of a rock. But the stonings I've seen, well, I've had nightmares for quite a while afterwards. A stoning is not a pretty sight.

Better go on turning those stones into bread, Lord. The bread went down rather well when we were caught without a decent dinner last week. That pretty much proved you were the Son of the Living God, didn't it? And didn't we hear your very words, "If your child asks for bread will you give a stone?" Better go on turning those stones into bread, Lord.

Speaking of stones, I seem to remember reading somewhere that God's angels will come to the aid of God's chosen one so he will not dash his foot against a stone. This Jesus is God's chosen one. We have just figured that out. God's chosen one, therefore no stonings! Ah, it helps to know your scriptures at times like this.

On the other hand, we who are mere followers of God's chosen one probably ought to be on guard when it comes to our own safety. I'm not sure how far the promise extends. Being realistic, we should be ready to run at a moment's notice.

You'll see I've done my exegetical homework. I understand about rocks and stones. So it puzzles me when Jesus starts talking about carrying our cross. The cross is the Roman form of torture and intimidation. What's it got to do with an internal Jewish matter like blasphemy? Obviously, this talk of crosses is another one of his parables, those stories which have a kind of spiritual meaning. He doesn't mean anything about crosses as such. He's just talking about the burden we all have to bear for being honest and seeking the truth. But I reckon he would be better to talk about stones rather than crosses when he needs an image that will really hit his audience in the eye. Metaphorically speaking of course.

Proper 18
(Ordinary Sunday 23)
MATTHEW 18: 15-20

Weaker Brethren

*I*n 1 Corinthians chapter 8 and Romans 14 the apostle Paul tried to present a way by which those who do eat meat and those who don't eat meat could live in the same church. His solution was that those who reckon it is okay to eat meat offered to idols ought to refrain if it causes their brothers and sisters to stumble. So we interpret Paul's words and end up with the doctrine of "the weaker brethren," a totally unscriptural idea, as are many other harmless-sounding words and phrases we throw around having half-listened to God's word.

The idea of "the weaker brethren" is not biblical because Paul is not telling one group to feel superior and to label another group. It is not that we treat people as weaker brethren. Rather, if one group seems to be weak, then, says Paul, make sure you treat them as brothers and sisters. If we continue to insist on a worldlier than thou attitude, we might well ask who are really the weak ones. If I am free indeed I can give up my freedom for the sake of love.

With this in mind, not to mention the saying about the specks and logs, I am mindful of my penchant for spiritual pride as I point out the faults of others.

Even without the weight of so many other parts of scripture, the context of this passage from Matthew ought to alert us to the ease with which we pass from spiritual care to spiritual blackmail. Stop trying to decide who is greatest in the kingdom. To enter the kingdom we must be like children, unimportant nobodies. If we cause others to stumble, we will soon find ourselves with another sort of rock around our necks. Take care of the little ones like a shepherd with his sheep. Yes, Peter, forgive seventy times seven, in fact, stop counting altogether. We might get this whole forgiveness business into perspective with another parable.

Certainly, if this sinner, whom you are treating like a brother or sister, refuses to listen to you, let them become as a Gentile or a tax collector. But then stop for a moment and reflect on the place of Gentiles and tax collectors in this kingdom of heaven, in the church of Matthew's world. Have we forgotten so soon that our author himself was presented as a tax collector? Have we forgotten so soon that our Lord has recently been taken to task concerning his exclusivist attitudes and miracles by a pushy Canaanite woman?

While you are busy binding and loosing things with your newfound authority, take care that you do not bind yourself who have been set free by Christ. Take care that you do not loose your spiritual pride that wants to make everyone a carbon copy of you. Remember whose church this is, and who promised to build it.

No wonder you need to get together with two or three others to pray. It may just be your own soul you are asking for.

Proper 19
(Ordinary Sunday 24)
MATTHEW 18:21-35

❦

That Taught My Heart to Fear

*T*his is no way to reduce the Budget deficit, to go around forgiving people to the tune of fifteen years' wages. But this is what the kingdom of heaven is like. Such generosity is simply not realistic. Real life doesn't work like that. So we have a big problem because we who love Jesus are living in this world as those who belong to the kingdom of heaven.

I doubt if it is good exegetical method, but I can't help delving into the motives of the slave who was first forgiven, and the motives of the king who forgave him. Why on earth would anyone who has just been forgiven half a million dollars (a million with inflation) go straight out and accost someone else who owes a hundred dollars? Is this slave simply bad at arithmetic? No one, not even a generation of schoolchildren brought up on calculators, could be that bad. Has the recent encounter with the king slipped his mind? Surely the forgiveness would be still ringing in his ears. Why is he so vehement with such a small offender, so vehement that his fellow slaves found it necessary to speak to the king about it?

Martin Luther once said of the story of our Lord's Passion, "No part is so carefully portrayed as Peter's denial, and there is a good reason, for no article is so hard to believe as the forgiveness of sins."

It is hard to believe in the forgiveness of sins because we don't really like God's grace and mercy. You'll remember that Jonah sat under the bean plant at Nineveh and sulked because God was merciful. In the words of the prophet himself, "That is why I fled to Tarshish at the beginning; for I knew that you are a gracious God, slow to anger and abounding in steadfast love..." It would have made more sense for Jonah to say that his God is an angry and jealous God. It is God's grace that really gets up the prophet's nose.

It is hard to believe in grace and mercy and complete forgiveness because the world is not like that. When the king wants to be gracious, it makes us mad enough to go out and punch someone else on the nose... or demand they pay back the hundred dollars they owe.

I was once so annoyed by God's grace after a sabbatical year in which I felt de-skilled by not having a lot to do, that I wrote this poem:

SABBATICAL GRACE

I'm sick to death of bloody grace!
I've spent a whole year being still.
"The silence is God's gift," they say,
And so I've bowed my mind and will
And held the gift and waited till
The silence taught me how to pray:

And now I tell you, face to face,
I've bowed my body, not my mind.
This grace is not enough for me.
(Forgive me if I seem unkind.)
I'm made to work, to chase the wind.
I cannot simply sit and be.

So free me from your tight embrace
And let me loose to till the earth
With Adam, Eve, and, yes, with Cain,
Through lonely thorns and painful birth,
And let me find in work some worth....
...Until I need your grace again
And come back to this garden place.

Proper 20
(Ordinary Sunday 25)
MATTHEW 20:1-16

It Wasn't Meant to be Fair

I always take great delight in introducing people to this particular parable for the first time. They are taken in by the passing of the working day and the growing desperation of the owner. I can still recite most of the rhyming version from the old Arch Books which our children insisted we read a hundred times over. "It's Hector your helper," a timid voice said... for the third, fourth, and fifth time. And so Sir Abner the owner gets out of bed and goes back to the marketplace to hire some more workers.

When the ending finally arrives, it catches listeners by surprise and they often cry out in disgust, "But that's not fair."

C.S. Lewis has written a marvelous poem around the same theme, in which he loses his lover to a Johnny-come-lately. Next his literary skill is spurned by the Muses in favor of an untrained country bumpkin. He finally turns to God and excels at religious duty only to find "a ne'er-do-well who smelled of shag and gin" welcomed into heaven before him. At last he sees the joke and joins Balaam's Ass in the meadows singing the "Donkey's Delight." [1.]

The story of the Workers in the Vineyard is not fair because God is not fair, thank God.

Jesus has warmed up for another round of parables for those who travel with him. They are on the home straight to Jerusalem now and the third prediction of the Passion is approaching. When things get desperate he turns to stories, stories that shock us out of our complacency. These stories picture a world that is familiar to the hearers. Everyone understands about casual laborers and landowners. The latter are always trying to rip off the former, and the former lead a precarious existence waiting in the marketplace and trying to look nonchalant about a job.

The proponents of the "new hermeneutic" reckon that with a parable such as this, Jesus stands alongside his listeners in the marketplace. Ernst Fuchs says, "Is this not the way of true love? Love does not just blurt out. Instead it provides in advance the sphere in which meeting takes place." [2] However, the love of Jesus is no mere sentimental feeling. These stories open up a world of possibility. Once the hearer is inside the story they are challenged about their deepest beliefs and assumptions about the world. This parable of grace grasps us at a deeper level than a mere illustration or example. It is a language event. It is God being generous. Within this story God asks me, "Friend, I am doing you no wrong...are you envious because I am generous?"

Thus in the telling of this story, the kingdom of God is among us. And it is not fair at all. Thank God.

1. C.S. Lewis *Poems*, Geoffrey Bles, London, 1964, 29-31.

2. A.C. Thiselton *The Two Horizons*, The Paternoster Press, Exeter, 1980, 345.

Proper 21
(Ordinary Sunday 26)
MATTHEW 21:23-32

❦

Good Things Come in Threes

I have already said somewhere that you should not make parables into allegories where each element in the parable world stands for something in our world. But with some parables it is very tempting: God is the landowner, the bridegroom, or the parent. I am the slave, the virgin, or child.

When you are invited into today's particular parable-world, it is tempting but very hard to decide which side to take. Well of course we are on the side of the son who said he would obey his dad and go work in the vineyard. Except that he didn't go. So we'd better not be like him. After a while we think of taking the side of the son who actually does go and work in the vineyard. Except that he is a pretty poor specimen too because he was rather rude at the start and his deeds don't match up with his words. That mismatch is fortunate in the end, but he is in reality only another kind of hypocrite.

Matthew also appears to succumb to the temptation to allegorize and makes it sound as if the Pharisees who rejected John the Baptist were like the son who said no. The tax collectors and prostitutes would therefore be the children who say yes and then fail to live up to their promises. We can see that such an interpretation is getting pretty messy, if not plain wrong. We are used to parables that take the side of the sinners. And in the end parables like the Prodigal Son make us glad to be gentiles, outsiders, sinners, because we can be assured of our entry ticket no matter what wicked things we get up to in the meantime.

In all the interpretations attempted so far there is definitely something missing. Some ancient manuscripts see the problem and try to find the missing link and repair the damage. They change the order of the sons, or they even answer that the son who merely says the right thing gets his father's approval!

Could it be that we have been asking the wrong questions of this text all along? The text has been patient with our fumbling for answers that meet our own pitiful standards of truth, and fulfil our meager expectations of love and justice. But parables are not here to fulfill our expectations. So we must return to this text and listen again. The problem is solved if we cease to equate mere words (Yes, I will go) with belief (I believe in John the Baptist). If we understand doing the will of the father as equivalent to believing then the problem of identification is solved.

The point is that in order to complete this story there really ought to be a third son. These stories do often go in threes. With the third son, the believing and the going, the words and the deeds, will match up and show that he is a true child of his father. Just to show that he does know what he is doing after all, Matthew provides us with just such a story immediately following this one.

Proper 22
(Ordinary Sunday 27)
MATTHEW 21:33-46

❧

On Rocky Ground

*W*hen you go to Israel, especially to the hills around Jerusalem, the most impressive thing is the rocks. I even found myself humming an old rock (!) song:

"I've got rocks, rocks, rocks in my head
and the rocks keep rolling around."

You can tell Jesus is getting desperate in this last week. The parables are coming thick and fast now. "Listen," he says, and there is plenty of scope for listening, putting old images together and coming up with new ones. These people already know about vineyards and owners. It can be a tricky business starting a vineyard in this rocky ground and it is definitely a long-term venture.

Sensible landowners put up fences. It is two birds with one stone, so to speak. You clear the fields of rocks so the vines can grow and you make a wall of the rocks to keep out undesirables. The wine press and the watchtower will also be made of rocks. And still there will be stones left over for building kingdoms and churches, or for stumbling over and being crushed.

Sensible landowners also make demands on their tenants, even before the land produces wine, so that the tenants cannot claim there is no such thing as an owner except themselves. If the tenants can keep such claims at a distance, they may be able to show legally that they own the vineyard. The rocks come in handy once again for keeping out those human reminders of the owner.

It is somewhat less than sensible for the landowner to send a son. It would be better to send an army against these miserable wretches. When it comes to rounding off the story, the listeners are happy to provide a bad ending for bad tenants. It reminds me of King David's reaction to Nathan's parable. The difference is that, when David realized the parable was about him, he repented.

We chief priests and Pharisees are a little quicker at pointing our finger at others, and slower in realizing the story is about us. We prefer to see ourselves standing outside the story, perhaps as members of the crowd who believe Jesus is a prophet and thus save him from being stoned today. Or we see ourselves as members of a newly constituted vineyard, where we would most certainly give due credit to the landowner. We would use the watchtower to spot enemies, not servants of the owner. We would build the walls only high enough to keep out the foxes, not the son.

"Listen," says Jesus in his desperation to be heard before it is too late. "Listen to another parable, and another, and another." So we are invited to enter the stories that Jesus tells, not to invent our preferred version. Where are we in this vineyard? Where are we in relation to this owner? There are still many rocks rolling around the field and the rocks are more dangerous to us than to them.

Proper 23
(Ordinary Sunday 28)
MATTHEW 22:1-14

RSVP

I have noticed that weddings often bring out the worst in people. People mostly behave themselves in church, but I have been to wedding feasts where the alcohol loosened manners to breaking point. I think weddings bring out the worst because the bride and groom are ostensibly so happy that everyone else realizes they are not quite as happy as all that. People crack under the pressure of the moment, even when it is meant to be a festive occasion.

Perhaps that is why people have refused to come to this great occasion. But I cannot see any reason for slaughtering those who brought the invitations. When the king throws out a poor fellow just because he didn't know what "black tie" meant, we begin to suspect that this is not a realistic story. On the other hand weddings do bring out the worst in people, even in the parents of the happy couple.

Since Jesus' story is more vicious than your average wedding, more than a TV soap opera wedding, we superior commentators on the text begin to slice up the story and name only the nicer bits as original. When this story first came together there would have been plenty of time to slice it up. When our author picked up his pen and papyrus for the final draft, he saw fit to keep it intact. Scribes ever since have done their best to hold it together. It thus seems presumptuous of twentieth century readers to tear the parable apart again. But weddings do bring out the worst in people.

This is another of Jesus' parables that we chop and change at our peril. Last week there was the vineyard to work in. We might have preferred another vineyard further along the hill, but it would not have been the vineyard Jesus was talking about. There is now a wedding feast to attend. There are probably minor weddings going on all the time too, but we are being invited to a huge affair with Jesus. It is so big that whole oxen and calves are being slaughtered and black tie is mandatory. Perhaps this wedding brings out the worst in people because it is so important. The king wants to get it exactly right because it is forever.

So, having decided to come in to exactly this wedding feast, we are now being invited to lounge around the hall and nibble savories until the bridegroom arrives. When the king comes in to see us I hope he will not look too closely at the sherry I spilt on my sleeve, or notice that I did not shine my shoes this morning. I wish I had found time to get to the hairdresser this week. The king wants to get it exactly right for his son. That's why he sent the slaves out to get people like me, in order to fill the hall. He may now prefer to have fewer guests in order to have the right guests.

The question is whether we really want to come to this feast in the first place, whether we want to take the risk. A wedding feast as big as this one is not for the fainthearted.

Proper 24
(Ordinary Sunday 29)
MATTHEW 22:15-22

Amazing Images

*I*n the preceding parable there was man who was speechless when the great king asked him a question. These people around Jesus are not speechless. Not yet. They are even talking to each other. Wondrous unity is being forged between opposing parties. They have a common enemy and they are setting out to trap him. They have some questions for the teacher.

Money, politics, ultimate allegiances, all combine to make a good trap. The trap is baited with false flattery, but Jesus is not fooled. The image on the coin is that of the emperor. So the coin presumably belongs to the emperor. Give it back to the one who owns it.

Give also to God the things that are God's. Where is the image of God that I may give that coin back to the one who owns it? "God created humankind in his image, in the image of God he created them; male and female he created them." Give back to God what belongs to God.

Each of us Pharisees and Herodians could give our lives back to the living God. That would be a good thing in itself, but it is not quite what is meant by the image of God. The image is not in each of us as individuals. It is in humankind, male and female, people together, imaging God's own diversity.

By accident or malice, these Pharisees and Herodians almost had it right, coming together in their diversity as human beings. They definitely did have it right in the one they chose to come to, but they have come for the wrong reason. The trap they had hoped to spring for Jesus has scattered them to their own corners of the vineyard. From there they will make a last foray or two but it will be on their own, royalists or republicans, far right or hard left. Unity around a common enemy is a false unity and it does not last very long. The image of God is fading fast.

At the end of this conversation they will go away and they will not come together again, except perhaps to see their handiwork on the cross. Even then there will be a chance. This Jesus around whom they have gathered today could, in his death, bring them together again as the image of God on earth. This Jesus is the only individual of whom it can be said, "He is the image of the invisible God... for in him all the fullness of God was pleased to dwell... You who were once estranged and hostile in mind, doing evil deeds, he has now reconciled in his fleshly body through death."

In a strange twist of fate, as they gather at the cross, they do give back to God the one true image of God, the man Jesus. As they come together to see one cursed and rejected by God, they could become the image of God, far right and hard left, male and female, rich and poor, the body of Christ. They need only come and then they will be truly amazed.

IN YOUR IMAGE

You have made us in your image
So we long to see your face,
Sisters, brothers, all, your children,
Searching till we find our place.

You have made us in your image
And we long to move as one.
As a body, crossing frontiers,
Traveling on to meet the Son.

You have made us in your image
So we have diversity.
Different journeys, but accepting
Others' journeys joyfully.

You have made us in your image,
People always on the move,
Daring wilderness and desert,
Motivated by your love.

You have made us in your image.
Guide us daily by your hand;
Make us bold to cross new frontiers;
Bring us to the Promised Land.

Proper 25
(Ordinary Sunday 30)
MATTHEW 22:34-46

❧

Hear, O Israel

*I*t is often said that the first and great commandment is a kind of summary of the first four of the Ten Commandments, namely the ones to do with God. The second commandment given by Jesus is, then, a summary of the last six, those to do with our neighbor. I have used this distinction myself for teaching purposes, but even as I have said it, I realized it is not quite so simple a distinction.

Parents, murder, adultery, theft, false witness, and coveting are undoubtedly to do with our relationship with other people. Having other gods, making images, and taking God's name in vain are ostensibly about our relationship with God. But what about the sabbath commandment? Is this one about God or neighbor? It is a sabbath "to the Lord," but it says much about fairness for slaves and aliens. On the other hand, its basic thrust is not that we should do anything on this one day in seven, not even strive for social justice, but that, like God, we should cease from doing. If loving is an action word, what is this commandment that sits so quietly between God and neighbor?

The commandment to keep the sabbath looks back to God's work and perfection, in creation in the Exodus version of the Ten Commandments, and in rescue from slavery in Egypt in the Deuteronomy version. It looks forward to justice and shalom for the community. But just between God and neighbor is a quiet space, a space to do precisely nothing, to stop trying so hard.

It is this turning point between the commandments that has thrown the opponents of Jesus. They only asked for one great commandment and they got two. The more religious might be glad to hear the first commandment, the activists might prefer to hear the second. But in putting them together, likening them, setting them as the basis of all the law and the prophets, now that has set the cat among the pigeons.

It is amazing that a commandment about doing nothing can be so socially radical, but prophets like Isaiah and Amos fiercely agree about the centrality of sabbath-keeping. Perhaps it is because when we cease from our work we are like everyone else, we are equal. When the banks close, when the shopkeepers put up the shutters, when even the slaves sit down, everyone is in their proper place, as human beings made in God's image and redeemed by God's mighty hand and outstretched arm. The sabbath reminds us that the distinctions we set up between human beings are only temporary.

That is why the second is like the first. We are who we are when we sit still, because God is God even when he is not running around arranging the universe. It is difficult to sit still. It can be mistaken for sheer laziness. It has been mistaken for indifference on God's part. But it is a matter of survival, a matter of salvation, that we realize Descartes was wrong: I do not think therefore I am. I sit still and I listen, therefore I am. *

*Walter Brueggemann *Finally Comes the Poet: Daring Speech for Proclamation*, Fortress Press, Minneapolis, 1989, 82.

The Old, Old Story

*T*he Scribes and the Pharisees have recently run away from Jesus and his discerning questions and answers. They are not therefore dismissed by Jesus as they have dismissed him, for they sit on the seat of Moses. They are the ones who make the connections with the ancient story. They bridge the gap of hundreds of years from the time of the great teacher and leader to today. The Scribes and Pharisees are therefore a necessary part of the story itself. We cannot tell a completely new story apart from them. Not even Jesus can tell a completely new story. Jesus is not starting a new religion, but following in the very line of Moses and the prophets. So Jesus says to the crowds and to his disciples, concerning those very ones who refused to listen to him, "Do whatever they teach you. Listen to them."

Where is it that the Pharisees have gone wrong? Is it that they do not practice what they preach? Are they mere hypocrites who say one thing and do another? They follow the Law of Moses in minute detail. They preach hard things and then go out and do hard things, encouraging their disciples to follow.

The trouble with the Pharisees is rather, like religious people, that they try too hard. Their good works are broad and their theological discussions are long. They enjoy their religion and the enjoyment shows in their dress, in their social graces. Much as I enjoy long theological discussions, much as I delight in goodness spread abroad, this kind of religion is laying intolerable burdens on people. It may well be that Christianity is not a religion at all, if religion is about human beings trying to reach out for God. Christianity is not about trying hard. It is not about passing exams or pleasing a taskmaster. Christianity is about God reaching to us, from the seat of Moses.

The ancient story was first told by a woman dancing and playing her tambourine by the seashore. Miriam sang about freedom from slavery, about oppressors who were held under water until they drowned from their own need to put burdens on others. Those who teach from the seat of Moses should be terrified to think their version of the story has made them like the Egyptian oppressors. There are no fathers but one, no instructors but God, no pharaohs, no burdens, no religion.

If the Pharisees truly understood their responsibility in passing on the story of Moses, they would let the story itself continue to shatter established religion as it had always done in the past. They do not need to try harder to find deeds to match their words. They need to listen to their own words, listen to the old, old story which makes all things new, and have their tidy religiosity shattered and made new. That is the hardest burden to place on anyone and it ought to be left to God to place. It took one such Pharisee from Tarsus quite a few years in the wilderness to pick up the pieces of his shattered theology. When he did sort it out, his preaching changed the world, preaching that began from the ancient seat of Moses.

Proper 27
(Ordinary Sunday 32)
MATTHEW 25:1-13

❦

Oil in My Lamp

*I*n these last days there have been enough warnings to "Keep awake". The Son of Man is coming. The bridegroom is delayed, but will come soon. Keep awake. Be watchful. Nevertheless when it comes to the crunch, we will note the strange fact that the closest friends have fallen asleep in the garden just when their Master needed them most. Strange that the main story will head towards a point where the Son of Man himself, the bridegroom, will sleep for three days in a bed of stone. Strange that later on in this story the guard at the tomb will use the excuse that they were fast asleep when the body disappeared, and their story is still told to this day.

It is not that anyone is to be blamed for falling asleep. God made the day and night. God made the sabbath rest and entered into the rest himself. No one can be blamed for sleeping in the middle of the night. That is the time to sleep. It is rather that preparations can and should be made before bedtime, while it is still day. The foolish girls could have brought enough oil. The wise girls are not to be despised because they did not share their oil. Just enough oil cannot be made into extra oil simply because one person feels sorry for another. (Unless you happen to be Elijah or a prophet.)

As they prepare, the ten girls need to get clear what it is they are waiting for, why they have their lamps burning, where the door will lead. If they really want to go in to the wedding feast, if they consider that the best thing that ever happened to them is that the bridegroom is on his way, they will be ready.

Strange that the three disciples will very soon fall asleep in the garden because they think they have had a feast with their Lord and do not realize it is only a taste of the banquet to come. Even if they had not mistaken a supper for a feast, they could never believe that the bridegroom's moment has come with a rude arrest, a trial, and a traitor's death. They could not in their worst nightmares imagine that the bridegroom will enter and the door will shut on all twelve disciples, whether asleep or awake. There are some things that this bridegroom must do alone. Tasting the bitterness of death, allowing the grave to swallow him, cannot be done on behalf of anyone else. (Unless you happen to be a prophet or the Son of Man.)

Strange that the guards at the tomb almost have it right when they claim to have been sleeping when the great moment arrived, for not one of the disciples can explain exactly what has happened at the tomb either. They only know what the authorities know, that the body is missing and some are saying the bridegroom is now walking around in Galilee. Strange that the foolish women are still hanging around the door to the wedding banquet and have been the first to notice in the morning light that the door now is wide open.

Proper 28
(Ordinary Sunday 33)
MATTHEW 25:14-30

❧

What Will You do if You Win?

*W*hat a windfall. They tell me that this fellow has been given fifteen years' worth of wages. True, his friends have been given thirty and seventy-five years' worth of wages, nevertheless he cannot sniff at the smaller amount. It is a huge sum of money. But he knows it is not really his. He knows that the one who has given it to him intends to return one day and will want to settle accounts.

This story of the three slaves sets aside our usual ideas about work and labor. It is not that the man going on a journey has left us to get about our own business and will one day return to see how hard we have worked. It is not even that we have each been given a shovel and told to dig in our corner of the field as the first human being was set to work in the beautiful garden. We who live in the new creation have been given the fruits of labor, the final product, between seventy-five and fifteen years' worth of wages in fact, as a gift. It is not unlike winning the lottery. What will you do if you win?

I read once some follow-up studies of people who had won large amounts of money in the soccer pools. The study discovered that, a few years after their windfall, they were not really any happier. In fact, there was a good case for saying that the winners were less happy than your average loser. The huge sums of money changed their lives for the worse. They went on ridiculous spending sprees and ended up completely broke, or they became miserly and became less than human. It is truly more blessed to give than receive, but it is also harder to receive than to give.

There are odd discrepancies in this Gospel story. There is a discrepancy between the description of the winners as slaves and yet they are able to make huge monetary transactions. These winners are called slaves, for so they are, but they are treated like stockmarket traders. They have been given a gift with which to have fun. Two of them take the chance and have fun, acting as financial entrepreneurs, making more talents as a result. The one whose basic motivation is fear has the money to return to his master, but nothing else, and so he loses the little he has. "Here is your money," he says, "your money," when the master has already given notice that the money is to be regarded as belonging to the slave. The slave continues to think like a slave and his obstinate refusal to look a gifthorse in the mouth becomes his downfall.

The others have taken their windfall and learnt to think as free people. They are commended, not for the amounts they have produced so much as their attitude to the money in the first place. They who have enjoyed acting as owners are invited in to share the happiness of the one who is the real owner. The slavish fellow cannot even think past his own efforts to deal with the money. In fear and trembling he digs a hole and hides the offending money bag. It may sound cruel to throw the offender out, but he has already shown he does not belong where freedom becomes reality.

Reign of Christ
(Ordinary Sunday 34)
MATTHEW 25:31-46

❧

Finding the Go in Gospel

*T*here have been many stories in this Gospel about people who did not know just how important their stories were. Bridesmaids did not realize how important the light really was. Servants did not understand that they were rich bankers. Religious leaders turned out to be the bad guys because they thought they were the good guys. Guests were and weren't invited to weddings, refused to come or were thrown out when they did come. Mostly negative stories, they had tragic endings. They were the kind of stories that Jesus could easily identify with, since he too had a tragic ending.

After the biggest story and truest tragedy of all time, the Master will give final instructions to his friends to go into all the world with good news. The world is where Matthew has been headed all this year we have spent in his company, into all the world. Those servants, financiers, tenants, owners, guests, bridesmaids, and pharisees can now go into all the world remembering that Jesus is with them always. In fact, they had better go or they may miss being with Jesus who has only promised to be with them out there, in all the world.

Where, Lord, can I find you? In the thirsty and hungry and needy and grubby and smelly and unlovely, says today's penultimate story. In the least expected places. It is not by chance that the priests and elders meet after the burial of our Lord and come up with a financial arrangement and another story, a bogus story. They plan to tell all the world that the disciples have come by night and have taken away the body of Jesus.

And ever since that first bogus story there have been financial arrangements and failures to go into all the world because the body of Jesus has indeed been removed by the disciples. It has been removed from all the world and put into lovely and expensive buildings that have the luxury of a deeply religious atmosphere. It has been removed from all the world and put into beautiful people who have the luxury of a deep and lasting faith. It has been removed from all the world and trapped in one or another culture and language. It has been removed from the thirsty and hungry and needy and grubby and smelly and unlovely, and been dressed in gold and jewels. Disciples who propagate such a false story deserve eternal punishment. They will shortly walk away into the night with the misguided Judas Iscariot, and they will make financial arrangements that are ultimately suicidal.

The disciples were told by an angel to go into Galilee if they wished to see the living Lord. Now they are told by the Lord himself to go into all the world. There is no other place that they can expect to find the body of Christ. Those who say otherwise are telling a false story and that is the biggest tragedy of all.

Postscript

🦂

Meanwhile Back in the Jungle...

I was driving along through the jungle
when I glanced in the rearview mirror.
(They say you should always glance in the rearview mirror,
even when traffic ahead is thick.
In case something creeps up on you from behind.)

I only meant a brief look—
but something caught my eye,
and I have been glancing in the mirror ever since.

I can no longer make much sense of the scenery ahead,
but the backward glance—
though I can never look for long—
is the one thing that seems clear to my mind.

I am confused by thoughts of mirrors,
and my mind can't get it straight.
 Can you look someone in the eye in a mirror?
 Am I the subject or the object of the looking?
Now I don't even know if I'm the driver of this car
or a backseat passenger.
I wish I had never looked in the mirror.
But I wouldn't give up the view for anything.